I Believe

The IVF Miracle We Prayed For, the Storm We Never Expected

JEFFREY W. WHEELER JR

To Sasha, my rock and firm foundation, and to Eliana, the precious gift God entrusted to us: No one could have navigated this pregnancy journey with more grace and strength than you, Sasha. Through two years of trying to conceive—supporting me through a vasectomy reversal, enduring heartbreak after a miscarriage, and holding on to faith when mine wavered—you reminded me daily to believe in God the Father, Christ the Son, and the Holy Spirit. You are the strongest person I know, both mentally and emotionally, and I could not ask for a more loving mother for Eliana or a better partner in life. You make me a better person every day.

To Josh and Sarah Sabol, dear friends, loving parents, and family in every way that matters: Josh, from college onward, you've been my best friend, my best man, my flying buddy, and my rock. Together, you and Sarah set an example of faith, resilience, and love that inspires me constantly. You've showered Eliana with gifts and supported us through every high and low. Having walked the IVF journey yourselves for my goddaughter, you truly understand the emotional roller coaster of pain, hope, and joy that comes with bringing a child into the world. Your steadfast belief in me, and in the power of faith, has propelled me forward through every challenge. You both embody everything parents and godparents should be.

To Chris McComb, my childhood and lifelong best friend: You have shown me the true meaning of friendship. You've been there at my best and at my worst, never wavering in your support—standing by my side when I needed a kickstand and forgiving me when I stumbled. Your upbeat spirit and personal successes have challenged me to become a better person every day. You taught me that a heart rooted in forgiveness doesn't dwell on the past—a truth echoed in a lyric from Cory Asbury's "Sparrows." I wouldn't be who I am without you.

To my parents, whose love and support laid the foundation for my faith and perseverance: You instilled in me the values of hard work, kindness, and unwavering devotion. From my earliest memories, you have been a wellspring of encouragement, cheering me on through every dream and challenge. Your belief in me, coupled with your constant prayers and guidance, shaped me into the person I am today. I am forever grateful for your enduring love and wisdom.

Finally, to God, who brought each of these remarkable people into my life: When I hit rock bottom, You led me to new hope through Christian music, through the words and melodies that inspired these pages. This book is Your story, and I am simply the vessel who put pen to paper. I dedicate this work, and all that I am, to You.

Copyright ©2025 Jeffrey W. Wheeler, Jr. All rights reserved.

ISBN: 979-8-218-89301-9 (paperback)
ISBN: 979-8-218-89307-1 (ebook)

CONTENTS

Foreword	i
Preface	iii
Chapter One: The Beginning of You	1
Chapter Two: Progress and Pride	5
Chapter Three: The Tough Days	9
Chapter Four: A Rollercoaster of Hope	11
Chapter Five: The Trigger Point	15
Chapter Six: The Turning Point	17
Chapter Seven: Signs and Guidance	21
Chapter Eight: Faith over Fear	23
Chapter Nine: A Sparrow's Message	27
Chapter Ten: Visions and Connections	31
Chapter Eleven: Tears of Triumph—A Glimpse of Grace	35
Chapter Twelve: Anticipation and Adjustments	41
Chapter Thirteen: The Beginning of Forever	45
Chapter Fourteen: Trials and Tribulations	49
Chapter Fifteen: A Storm of Emotions and a Ray of Hope	55
Chapter Sixteen: Our First Vacation as a Family of Five	61
Chapter Seventeen: Hello, Little One	67
Chapter Eighteen: Growing Together	69
Chapter Nineteen: Twelve Weeks and Our Big Reveal	73
Chapter Twenty: Stubborn Little Kicks	77
Chapter Twenty-One: The Big Reveal and a Stormy Surprise	81
Chapter Twenty-Two: Warrior Mom and Our Growing Peach	87
Chapter Twenty-Three: Strength in the Struggle	93

Chapter Twenty-Four: My Sweet Little Avocado	97
Chapter Twenty-Five: Through the Fire	101
Chapter Twenty-Six: Half-Baked and Fully Loved	105
Chapter Twenty-Seven: Weathering Storms with Grace and Grit	109
Chapter Twenty-Eight: Feeling the Kick	113
Chapter Twenty-Nine: A Promise of Joyful Christmases to Come	115
Chapter Thirty: Celebrating Milestones Amidst Unexpected Twists	119
Chapter Thirty-One: Persevering Through the Pandemic's Echoes	123
Chapter Thirty-Two: Running on Faith, Not on Emergency Heat	127
Chapter Thirty-Three: Strength in the Waiting	131
Chapter Thirty-Four: Waves and Wonders	135
Chapter Thirty-Five: Embracing the Final Stretch with Faith	141
Chapter Thirty-Six: Holding Our Breath, Trusting Our Faith	145
Chapter Thirty-Seven: The Dawn of Your Arrival	153
Chapter Thirty Eigh: "God Has Answered— I Believe"	163
Our Blended Family Tree	171

FOREWORD

This book is a testament to faith—the kind of faith that moves mountains, breaks through despair, and ushers in miracles. It is a story of love, of resilience, of a promise whispered in quiet moments of hope and answered in God's perfect timing.

To Sasha, my love, and Eliana, my daughter, this journey belongs to you.

For over two years, our hearts carried the weight of longing. We dreamed, we prayed, and we endured the trials that come with wanting something so deeply that it becomes woven into the fabric of your soul. We faced months of disappointment, the aching silence of unanswered prayers, and the devastation of loss. But through it all, we clung to faith: Faith in each other, faith in God's plan, and faith that He had not forgotten us.

This book is more than a memoir; it is a chronicle of belief in the unseen; the journey of two people who refused to let go of God's promises. It is about the tears shed in the stillness of the night and the quiet strength of a woman who bore the weight of every injection, every doctor's appointment, every moment of uncertainty with unwavering courage. It is about a father who, though often at a loss for words, found his deepest love expressed in the waiting, in the hoping, in the steadfast commitment to seeing this dream fulfilled.

Eliana, you were always meant to be. Your name was written in the stars before we even knew you. Every step, every hardship, every song we sang in faith—especially Phil Wickham's "I Believe"—led us to you. And now, as you grow within your mother, as we prepare to meet you, we reflect on the incredible path that brought us here.

This book is not just for us. It is for the couples still waiting, for the parents who are holding on to fragile hope, for anyone who needs to be reminded that God's promises are not empty words. If our story reaches even one soul who is losing faith, then every word has served its purpose.

To our parents, our friends, and the countless hands that held us through this journey, we thank you. And to you, dear reader, may this book remind you that miracles are real, faith is worth fighting for, and love—when placed in God's hands—is never wasted.

With all my heart,

Jeffrey

PREFACE

Why I Wrote This Book

The summer of 2018 was the beginning of my darkest season. I walked out of my home and into what became a nearly three-year battle—a protracted divorce that drained me emotionally, spiritually, and physically. When people speak of *hitting rock bottom*, I don't claim to understand every story, but I do know what it looked like for me. I saw how dark it could get. I spent three days in a hospital, unable to speak to my son—and missed his birthday. I left my home in June 2018 with almost nothing: no access to the house I owned, no possessions, and a heart hollowed by grief. And yet, through the grace of God and the unwavering strength of my family, I found the will to take another step forward.

In the midst of that brokenness, I attended yet another court hearing. Afterward, my attorney—seeing how worn I was—invited me to dinner. Over stale bread and lukewarm coffee, we strategized our next move. When I left the restaurant, night had fallen. I stopped at a gas station on the edge of town. Under the harsh glow of the pumps, I took a deep, unsteady breath and prayed aloud:

"Lord, I'm tired of fighting. This battle is Yours now. I believe that if I stay in the boat, even through the fiercest storm, You will guide me to calm waters."

That moment of surrender—standing alone beneath the hum of fluorescent lights—was the hinge on which my life would turn.

Six months later, I met Sasha. Even in my storm-tossed life, she became my anchor. Her laughter broke through my despair; her faith reminded me that storms end. With her by my side and the Holy Spirit in our hearts, I dared to imagine a future again.

About three months after meeting Sasha, my attorney abruptly withdrew from my case. At first, it felt like another blow—but it became my first true test of faith. *Could I trust God when every earthly ally walked away?* I had no choice but to believe—in myself, and in Him.

Over the next two years, our relationship deepened. In the spring of 2022, I planned something special. With my heart full of hope, I proposed to Sasha during a trip to Annapolis, Maryland. It was more than just a proposal—it was a promise, not just to Sasha but also to our children: Colton (CJ), my son from a previous marriage; and Warren, Sasha's son from a prior engagement, whom I affectionately call Dave. That night, over dinner by the water, I asked the three of them to become a family with me.

From that point forward, we began building our lives as a blended family. Though the path was sometimes messy, the love was always real. These two boys, while not biologically siblings, grew to be brothers in every meaningful way. Through parenting, co-parenting, and the unique challenges of combining households, we learned to lean on grace, patience, and each other.

It was during that same night—joyful and full of possibility—that Sasha and I first talked about expanding our family. It wasn't a rushed conversation, but one that came from a place of healing and shared faith in the future God was building for us.

We dreamed of a child of our own, but seven years earlier, I had chosen a vasectomy. After much prayer and discernment, we decided on a reversal in June 2022. Miraculously, Sasha became pregnant almost immediately. But our joy was short-lived—a chemical miscarriage ended the pregnancy before it truly began. The ache of that loss was sharp, but our faith did not waver. Month after month, for twenty-three long months, we clung to hope through every negative test.

Mentally and emotionally, we struggled. We tried homemade IUI kits, injections, supplements, endless prayers, yet nothing seemed to work. We wrestled daily with questions we couldn't answer: *Why this struggle? Why such long waits?* But we knew one thing—for better or worse, this was God's timing, not ours. Only He knew when and how our child would come into being.

Finally, after nearly two years, we decided to pursue *in vitro* fertilization. At that decision, I saw a flame of excitement light up in Sasha's eyes—the first real spark of hope in ages. She told me repeatedly that she wanted to document every step: the shots, the scans, the prayers. She showed me Facebook and Instagram reels of couples chronicling their journeys and said, "I want to do the same."

One evening, as I drove home from work, I realized it wasn't enough to simply record this journey online. I wanted to go deeper. I wanted our daughter—once she arrived—to understand every sacrifice her mother made to bring her into the world. I wanted her to see, in living color, how God answered our prayers despite the odds.

And so, this book was born.

I Believe is more than a memoir of heartbreak, injections, and medical charts. It is a collection of letters—love notes—to our daughter, Eliana, that reveal her mother's unwavering courage, her father's steadfast faith, and the miracle of a promise fulfilled. To anyone walking through the wilderness of infertility: May you find in these pages the same mustard-seed faith that moved the mountain in our lives.

Because through every trial, every tear, and every unanswered question, we learned this irrefutable truth: When you place your hope in God's timing, miracles become inevitable.

CHAPTER ONE

THE BEGINNING OF YOU

May 3, 2024

Eliana, your story begins on a significant day—May 3, 2024, also the birthday of my oldest sister, Nicole. I had just returned from a flight for United Airlines the day before—one of the many trips that come with being a pilot—and your mom and I, each with our own plans for the day, knew we would reunite in the evening to start the incredible process of bringing you into our lives.

Even though we each started our morning separately, I could feel a sort of electric anticipation. Deep down, I knew that after all our praying and waiting, something life-changing was about to begin. Every small errand, every moment of routine, seemed charged with the knowledge that we were on the cusp of a miracle.

The day was a Friday. After saying goodbye to Dave and sharing some M&Ms and mint cookies and cream Hershey bars I picked up on my travels, I began my morning. Don't worry, my little one, I'll pick up treats for you too.

While your mom worked for a few hours, I was at home, mowing the lawn and cleaning the pool we had just opened for the season. Later, your mom took a short break to enjoy a facial, pampering herself in preparation for what lay ahead.

I remember looking up at the sky while mowing. The sun was warm, but not blistering—the kind of spring day that makes you thankful for new beginnings. I let my mind wander to thoughts of you, picturing a day when you'd be big enough to run around this yard yourself. I prayed, in my own quiet way, that God would guide us—through every high, every low, every unknown.

In the evening, we drove to Baltimore, shared a wonderful dinner at Kona's, and then attended a concert by Phil Wickham at the Lyric. The concert was named "I Believe," a name that resonated deeply with us given what we were about to undertake. Surprisingly, we found ourselves in the second row, swept up in the music and the moment.

Something about hearing the words of "I Believe[1]" felt like a direct message to our hearts. It was as if each lyric stitched together the hope and faith we'd been clinging to for so long. We closed our eyes, sang along, and I remember your mom squeezing my hand—both of us silently thanking God for the promise of you.

Returning home from the concert, we began the medical process necessary for your conception. Your mom and I had been trying to conceive naturally for nearly twenty-three months, enduring the heartache of a miscarriage in July 2022. It had been a long journey of hope and perseverance. That night, as we started with the IVF injections, our hearts were full of faith—a faith echoed by the theme of the concert we'd just attended.

It took a lot of faith from both of us to believe in this process. We placed our hopes and dreams in God's hands, trusting for a healthy and wonderful you.

There was a kind of hushed holiness in that moment—our bedroom lights dim, your mom gently preparing the syringe, and both of us whispering prayers under our breath. I recall thinking how surreal it was that the same God who carried us through our loss would also be

---

[1] Phil Wickham, "I Believe," written by Phil Wickham, Bethel Music Publishing / Fair Trade Music Publishing, 2023, track 1 on I Believe, *Fair Trade Services, 2023, MP3 audio.*

with us in this new chapter. I truly felt the words *I Believe* echoing in my mind, giving me courage every time doubt tried to creep in.

These notes, which will continue throughout our journey, will sometimes be long, sometimes short. They are my thoughts and feelings written down for you to read one day—perhaps when you're curious, or sad, or maybe even thinking about starting your own family.

I love you so much already, Eliana. I can't wait to meet you, to hold you, to spoil you, and yes, one day, to walk you down the aisle.

From that very first injection, we began to sense the powerful love God was pouring over our family. We dreamed big—of hearing your heartbeat for the first time, of rocking you to sleep, even of watching you take your first wobbly steps. Every prayer and every shot was a step forward in faith. That night, I closed my eyes and whispered, "I believe," letting the words settle in my heart with the sweet certainty that you were already so loved.

CHAPTER TWO

PROGRESS AND PRIDE

May 8, 2024

As we continue on this journey, today marks an important milestone, Eliana. We are on shot number six. The first two shots went very smoothly, and then I had to return to work—flying another trip for United Airlines—leaving your mom to manage the third and fourth injections by herself. I can't express how proud I am of how well she handled everything—her strength and bravery through this process are truly inspiring.

In those early days, I saw firsthand just how much your mom shoulders every single day. She juggles a full-time job, is a devoted mother to your brothers, and still found time to prepare the medications each evening. I remember one night she tried injecting the medication in her thigh, thinking it might spare her already-bruised belly—only to discover it hurt far worse. She told me later, in her usual calm voice, "I'll just stick to rotating spots on my stomach from now on," as though she hadn't just endured a wave of pain for your sake.

On Monday, your mom had her first doctor's visit where the news was encouraging. The doctors were pleased with how well her body is responding to the hormones. It's a testament to her resilience and the careful balance of science and hope that guides us.

Last night, we administered the fifth shot. Today, the medical team did bloodwork and an ultrasound, which showed nearly thirty eggs on her right side, measuring between thirteen millimeters to just less than nine millimeters. On her left side, there were eggs measuring thirteen millimeters, ten millimeters, and several smaller ones, all promising signs of a successful cycle.

Those initial few days of shots highlighted just how patient and faith-filled your mom truly is. Between her long work hours and caring for everyone at home, she would still stop in the middle of cooking dinner or helping with homework to measure out her injections. I'd catch her rubbing her sore belly afterward, quietly praying with each new bruise, reminding herself—and me—that through this discomfort, a dream was unfolding.

Today brought a change in your mom's medication regimen: We reduced the Follistim by half a dose and doubled the Menopur to two vials, or 150 units per day. Additionally, she started a seven-day course of Ganirelix. We are both filled with hope that the trigger shot could be any day now.

Your mom has been doing an incredible job, not just with the treatments but also in documenting this journey. She's been capturing these moments with photos that we'll share with you someday.

I think it's remarkable how, despite the pain, she still finds joy. She finishes a tough day, tucks your brothers in for the night, and then takes a quick moment to snap a photo of the medication boxes and her daily devotion. Seeing her brand-new bruises—and that determined smile—always reminds me how her faith lights up every room she walks into. She's independent and selfless, the kind of mother who would lay down her own comfort any time, for any child, especially for you.

I am overwhelmed with happiness and pride in how well your mom is doing, and how diligently she's preparing for your arrival. We both love you so much already, and each day brings us closer to the moment we can finally meet you.

It's clear that her patience, strength, and quiet faith are as vital to this process as the medications themselves. Day after day, she's forging ahead, giving everything she has so that one day soon, we'll hold you in our arms and whisper how very loved you are.

CHAPTER THREE

THE TOUGH DAYS

May 10, 2024

Eliana, every step of this journey brings its own set of challenges and emotions, and these past few days have been particularly tough. Yesterday marked day seven of the treatment. There wasn't a doctor's appointment, but it was a difficult day for your mom. The daily injections—sometimes up to three a day—are taking a toll on her. Her belly is bright red, and her arms are bruised from the frequent blood draws.

Some mornings, she wakes up wincing before her feet even hit the floor. I can see the exhaustion in her eyes, but she never once complains about the reason behind these bruises. It's as though every mark on her body is a badge of honor, reminding her of the promise she's holding onto: you.

Despite feeling unwell and emotionally drained, with noticeable bloating from the growing follicles, we managed to find a brief respite. We lay down around 12:30 and took an hour and fifteen-minute nap together, which seemed to lift her spirits a bit. However, earlier in the morning when I was administering her shots, she couldn't hold back her tears and expressed just how weary she was of the process. In my typical fashion, and struggling to show my deeper emotions, I responded with a smart-aleck comment, a flaw of mine that I need to fix, especially once you arrive.

Right then, I felt a pang of guilt—seeing her tears and the raw vulnerability etched into her face made me realize how deeply she needed reassurance, not humor. It struck me that this was not just her battle; it was ours. In that instant, I prayed silently that God would help me be the comforting presence she deserves, especially in these hardest moments.

Today, as we reach day eight, your mom is now required to go to the doctor daily. This morning, we learned more about the follicles, which need to measure between eighteen and twenty millimeters to ensure a mature egg is ready for retrieval. The doctor has increased the Follistim dosage from seventy-five milliliters to 150 milliliters per day, aiming for the best possible outcome.

Excitingly, we anticipate that the trigger shot might be administered as early as Sunday, with egg retrieval potentially scheduled for Tuesday or Wednesday. This timing is crucial, as I have a three-day trip starting Friday. While I'd gladly use sick leave to be with your mom, I hope to save that for when she needs me most, post-retrieval.

Despite the physical pain and emotional rollercoaster, seeing the follicles grow during the ultrasound appointments puts a big smile on your mom's face. It's a visual affirmation of her resilience and the tangible progress we're making toward meeting you. The pain she endures is a testament to her incredible strength and our shared dream of bringing you into our lives.

Whenever we catch a glimpse of those growing follicles, I'm reminded that each one carries a spark of hope. And in those brief moments of scanning lines on the ultrasound monitor, a sense of calm washes over us—a quiet assurance that every shot, every tear, and every prayer is bringing us one step closer to you.

We're full of hope and excitement, even as we navigate these new challenges daily.

CHAPTER FOUR

A ROLLERCOASTER OF HOPE

May 11 and 12, 2024

Eliana, these past couple of days have been a whirlwind of emotions and medical updates as we edge closer to a pivotal moment in our journey. Yesterday was shot number nine. We went to the doctor at 11:00 a.m., had blood drawn, and took more measurements of the follicles. When we left, your mom was in such a good mood. As we got into the car at exactly 11:30, Phil Wickham's "I Believe" played on the radio—a song that felt like a full circle moment[2] to me, a sign from God affirming our path.

Hearing that familiar melody drift through the car speakers felt like a divine nod to all the faith we've been pouring into this. Your mom, glowing despite her sore stomach and exhaustion, grinned at me. We both sat still for a moment, listening to the lyrics, letting them remind us why we keep believing so fiercely in you.

Later that day, the doctor called to reassure us that everything was progressing normally. He asked us to come in the next day—Mother's Day—for more bloodwork and another ultrasound. So, today, May 12, 2024, we spent about two hours at the doctor's office.

---

2   Ibid.

It wasn't an easy visit. The nurses were not in a great mood, and they were fairly rough during the blood draw, causing significant bleeding in your mom's left arm.

I remember watching your mom flinch as the nurse drew blood, and my protective instinct kicked into high gear. I wanted to shield her, to swap places if I could. But she just gave me a determined nod, letting me know she was okay and reminding me once more how strong she is—even on the days when she's worn down physically and emotionally.

Today's ultrasound showed mostly smaller follicles, around fourteen to fifteen millimeters, fewer than the twenty millimeters we were hoping for, which added a layer of worry. Despite this, we had a hopeful conversation on the way home. Tears filled my eyes as your mom discussed the fears and stories of others who've been through this—some without success and others facing heartbreak even after initial success. It's hard for me to show my emotions, but the possibility of another miscarriage after our past experiences is heart wrenching.

I tried to keep my voice steady, but I felt that familiar ache in my chest. In that vulnerable moment, it struck me how much courage it takes just to keep believing. Your mom never once wavered, though. She placed her hand on mine and whispered, "We have to keep praying, keep trusting." And somehow, hearing her say that gave me the strength to do the same.

Amid these fears, we received a call from the doctor while at the store. The news was better than expected: They decided to extend the treatment by one more day, with the trigger shot planned for Monday night and surgery on Wednesday. This news brought the biggest smile to your mom's face. Today being Mother's Day, it felt like the best possible gift we could have received.

We are ten days into this process, and it's visibly wearing on your mom. Each morning brings its own set of challenges and doubts, yet every piece of good news reignites the strength in her eyes. We're close to ending this chapter of the process, Eliana, and hopefully, tonight will be the last night of stinging shots. Let's pray that this next step brings us closer to you.

With each passing day, we lean more on our faith and on each other. Even in our toughest moments, we cling to the quiet assurance that God has brought us this far. Hearing that trigger shot was scheduled on Mother's Day, a date already brimming with significance, felt like a beautiful wink from above—a reminder that, in every up and down, He is weaving a greater story for our family. We believe you are the blessing waiting at the end of it.

CHAPTER FIVE

THE TRIGGER POINT

May 13 and 14, 2024

The culmination of weeks of hope, pain, and perseverance arrived on May 13. At 9:15 a.m., we were back at the doctor's office for what we hoped would be one of the last few visits of this phase. The ultrasound and bloodwork results were positive, and the doctors declared it was time for the trigger shot. This was the moment we had been waiting for, the final push before egg retrieval. The shot was scheduled for 10:45 p.m. that evening, and I administered it to Mom, marking the end of the injection phase and the beginning of a new, hopeful phase.

I still remember Mom looking at me with a mixture of triumph and relief when we got the news. We'd spent so many nights praying over every single injection, wondering if it would finally be enough. That morning, as we walked out of the clinic, it felt like every bruise, every tear, and every ounce of stress had led us right there—to the brink of something miraculous.

We were both elated, feeling a mix of relief and anticipation. The surgery was set for thirty-six hours later, on Thursday. It seemed that everything was aligning perfectly, with the procedure planned for a day when I would be home and not at work.

However, the journey took an unexpected turn the next morning. Mom woke up with a fever of 101.1 degrees Fahrenheit, feeling unwell—a side effect of the trigger shot, Lupron. It was a worrying development, but we hoped it wouldn't set us back. She immediately contacted the nurse, who reassured us that this was a known side effect and not uncommon.

Later that day, on May 14, the nurse called with reassuring news. After reviewing Mom's latest bloodwork, she confirmed that everything looked good. Her body had absorbed the medication effectively, and she was cleared for the egg retrieval that had been scheduled for the following day. This news lifted our spirits and renewed our hope.

Egg retrieval day was set and, as we prepared, our emotions were a tangle of nervous excitement and cautious optimism. We knew we were on the verge of a significant milestone, one that brought us closer to meeting you, Eliana. Despite the challenges, the strength and resilience we saw in each other provided a deep well of encouragement.

I can't fully describe how it felt to see Mom resting on the couch, shivering with a fever, and still managing a gentle smile. She whispered between ragged breaths, "We've come this far; God won't leave us now." That sentence replayed in my mind like a shield against all my fears. Even in physical discomfort, her faith lit up the room.

CHAPTER SIX

THE TURNING POINT

May 15, 2024

The sun hadn't yet washed away the morning chill when Mom and I, fueled by a mix of anticipation and nervous energy, left our quiet home behind. It was 8:45 a.m. The journey to Shady Grove Fertility felt shorter than usual, perhaps because every minute was weighted with what was at stake. By 9:15 a.m., we were stepping through the doors, Mom clutching a collection cup, her other hand holding a sign that declared, "Wake and pray, it's egg retrieval day"—a rallying cry for the day ahead.

Inside, the atmosphere was clinical, yet charged with an undercurrent of hope and fear. I watched as Mom was whisked away for surgery prep, leaving me in the echoing vastness of the waiting area, surrounded by other hopeful faces, each story interwoven with dreams of future laughter and tiny footsteps.

I spent much of that wait trying to quiet the hundred *what ifs* racing through my mind. *What if the procedure didn't go well? What if the eggs weren't viable?* In that restless moment, I silently recited the same prayer again and again: *God, please guide the doctor's hands, protect my wife.*

As they called me to join her, tension knotted in my stomach. In the prep room, the air was thick with the sterile scent of antiseptic; the walls, lined with charts and medical equipment, felt too close. I assisted Mom as she navigated the small indignities of pre-surgery routines. Suddenly, Dr. Doyle burst in, her expression taut with concern—she held the wrong chart. Confusion reigned for a heart-stopping moment before clarity returned and, with it, a renewed focus.

The wait during Mom's procedure was an abyss of time. I filled it by watching videos on the egg retrieval process, each clip a puzzle piece in understanding the intricate dance of science and miracle unfolding just beyond my reach. When they called me back, only twenty minutes had passed, but each second had stretched endlessly.

In the quiet of post-op, Mom's face, pale from anesthesia, slowly regained color. The nurse handed her crackers and water, simple comforts against the backdrop of our complex journey. Then came the news: thirteen eggs retrieved. A flicker of disappointment crossed Mom's features, quickly masked by resolve. Nurse Odette, sensing the shift, reassured us, "Eight to twelve is typical, but every journey is unique."

Later, Dr. Doyle explained a rare occurrence—Mom had ovulated an hour earlier than expected, impacting the count. Yet, as she spoke, it was clear: these thirteen eggs were our warriors in the fight for the future.

We left the clinic with mixed feelings, the day's highs and lows merging into a poignant blend of relief and contemplation. As we discussed, we realized that our journey—marked by this day of profound efforts and silent prayers—was not just about numbers. It was about faith; it was about one needed miracle.

In the car, I reached over for Mom's hand. She looked out the window, still foggy from the anesthesia, but with a gentle conviction in her eyes. "We have thirteen eggs," she said, "and that's thirteen more than we had yesterday." It hit me then how God's abundance sometimes shows up in ways different from what we first expect, but always enough for His purpose.

★ ★ ★ ★ ★ ★ ★ ★

CHAPTER SEVEN

SIGNS AND GUIDANCE

May 20, 2024

Today, Eliana, has been a day of stark contrasts: Deep sadness intertwined with budding hope. The news that my childhood best friend ended his battle with depression in such a tragic way has left me reeling. Throughout the day, as I flew, I struggled to contain a storm of emotions, trying my best to appear composed.

Knowing that shutting down wasn't the solution, I initially thought of confiding in Mom, who is always an incredible support. However, I felt a need for guidance from someone who could tap into a deeper understanding of the situation. So, I reached out to my friend Ann, who possesses a remarkable gift for clairvoyance. Through her tarot readings, she offered not just closure about my friend's passing without knowing the specifics but also insights that resonated deeply with me, providing a sense of comfort.

As our conversation shifted from my friend to personal updates, I mentioned how Mom and I had thought about naming a future son Maverick. But in a surprising twist during her card reading, Ann declared, "By the way, you're not going to have a boy; you're going to have a girl." Tears sprang to my eyes, as this revelation seemed to connect with everything we are hoping for with you.

Ann continued with her readings, pulling out three specific cards—the Nurture card, the Emperor card, and the Temperance card. Each card she described felt imbued with truth and sent waves of happiness through me. She suggested that Mom might benefit from exploring acupuncture or visiting a women's womb wellness center to cleanse any lingering negative energy.

Ann felt that your arrival would align somewhere between June and September, potentially leading to an April 2025 birthday. This timeline differs from our current expectation of a March birthday if everything with this first IVF attempt progresses as planned. It was a poignant reminder that we might need to prepare ourselves for the possibility that this first round may not go as hoped.

Later that evening, Mom and I discussed our emotional state and the need to be resilient for each other and for you. We talked about the importance of seeking signs from you, little signals that could guide us or show your presence in our lives. Ann had suggested asking for a sign, perhaps a yellow butterfly, but as I sat by the pool today, a mockingbird caught my eye—a swift, tiny bird darting among the flowers. It felt right, so I've chosen the mockingbird as the sign I'm hoping to see from you in the coming days.

Amid so much heaviness, I found myself asking God to help me stay open to His gentle nudges—whether through a bird, a dream, or a wise friend's words. This season of grief and hope felt like a testament to how life and loss often exist side by side.

This day has strengthened our bond and our resolve. Mom and I have never been stronger, and our readiness to welcome you into our world grows each day. I pray that we only have to go through this process once, and I ask for strength and health for Mom, and for you, my little girl, still just a cluster of cells growing far away but already so loved.

Eliana, I can't wait to meet you, to hug you, kiss you, and spoil you every day. I love you, little girl. I love your mom. I love our family.

CHAPTER EIGHT

FAITH OVER FEAR

May 22, 2024

Today unfolded under a brilliant sky, marking my first day off work after a bustling week. The lawn, unkempt and sprawling from the relentless spring rains, awaited my attention as I embarked on my chores. Yet, today's narrative isn't really about yard maintenance or the virtues of perfect lines in grass—though perhaps, Eliana, that's a story for another day.

As I navigated the jungle-like yard, Mom came outside, her presence underscored by a playful smirk and a telltale smudge of chocolate under her lip. Curiosity piqued, I powered down the mower to hear what she had to share. It was news from Shady Grove Fertility: Out of our seven embryos, three had survived. Mom's demeanor was light, her spirit undeterred by the numbers, embodying the superhero she truly is.

My initial reaction, however, mirrored the opposite. I felt a twinge of disappointment, my mind swirling with doubts about the odds of these three making it to the next stages—particularly about our chances of having you, my baby girl. But Mom, ever the beacon of positivity, quickly realigned my perspective. Her optimism was infectious, and as we talked a new resolve settled over me.

Standing there in the midday sun, I realized how vital her unwavering faith has become to me. No matter the stats or the doctor's calculations, she has repeatedly said, "God doesn't need big numbers to do big things."

Returning to my mowing, I slipped my AirPods back in and hit play on my music. The first song that greeted me was "Good Day" by Forrest Frank. I took it as a nudge from above, a reminder that today was indeed a good day, filled with promises and subtle signs to remain positive. We only need one strong embryo, after all.

As the blades of the mower churned through the grass, I reflected on our journey—on faith over fear. This isn't just about the embryos that didn't make it; it's about trusting that the ones that did are exactly what we need. Perhaps, in His wisdom, God is sparing us from making tough decisions, or maybe He's simply setting the stage for what's best for us.

This process, while daunting, isn't just a series of medical procedures; it's a spiritual journey. With Mom's upcoming spiritual session with Ann and the new *Spiritual Babies* book I've got lined up to read, we're leaning into every resource that can bolster our spirits and prepare us for whatever lies ahead.

I felt a quiet warmth spread in my chest, thinking about those three little survivors. Sometimes, a single spark of hope is all God needs to light up an entire future. I whispered a small prayer right there in the yard, thanking Him for guiding us this far.

Though I might not always show it outwardly—my emotions often masked by a stoic demeanor—inside, my heart is full of hope. Mom and I are fortified by a deep-seated belief that no matter how many attempts this journey demands, God will guide us to you, Eliana. Our faith in this process lights our path through any fear of failure or heartbreak.

We love you already, Eliana, and believe you're among the three embryos forging ahead. Your spirit is already so loved, and we are eagerly awaiting the day we can finally meet you.

CHAPTER NINE

A SPARROW'S MESSAGE

May 27, 2024

Eliana, is that you?

It's been a few days since I've written. Today, Memorial Day, we returned from a lovely weekend in Detroit with family—Nana W and Papa, Jenni and Nicki, and all our cousins, including Grammy Barb and her family. We cherished the warmth of family bonds, yet throughout the weekend, my mind occasionally wandered, searching for a sign I had asked for—a mockingbird. But now, I think I might have been mistaken in what I was looking for.

Secretly, all weekend, I kept an eye out for this bird. Yet, in a quiet moment of reflection, I wondered if what I really meant to look for was a hummingbird. I'm not sure why I initially thought of a mockingbird. Maybe it was a slip of the tongue, a miscommunication of the heart's true desire, which, as it turned out, might have been looking for something else—perhaps a sparrow.

After we arrived home, I dove into yard work, knowing I'd be away soon on back-to-back trips. The grass was already thickening after our recent rains, threatening to turn our yard into a wilderness once more. As I worked, a small sparrow flew into the garage. It darted about, making itself known, and didn't seem in any hurry to leave. I tried luring it out, saying softly, "Come on, little one, time to get out." But it stayed, almost as if it had something to tell or show me.

That's when it dawned on me—perhaps this was your spirit visiting. Maybe in asking for a hummingbird, what I was meant to find was this sparrow all along. I told Mom about it, saying half-jokingly, "I found Eliana, she's hanging out in the garage." We both tried to guide it toward the open door, yet it lingered. Finally, after some gentle persuasion, the sparrow seemed to decide it was time to go, but not before giving us a little scare by hitting the wall and tumbling down. Mom, ever so nurturing, rushed over to make sure it was okay. After a brief pause, the little bird picked itself up and flew off, strong and unharmed.

Reflecting on this, I remembered a song by Cory Asbury called "Sparrow," which I had once asked Mom to listen to closely.[3] The lyrics felt eerily relevant now: "The sparrow's not worried about tomorrow or the troubles to come . . . so why should I be? 'Cause you take good care of me."

That little sparrow, appearing out of nowhere, felt like a reassurance from God that He's watching over us. Every day, He cares for even the smallest bird; how much more, then, will He care for us? It was a timely, gentle reminder to keep our hearts open and trust His hand in every detail.

This encounter feels like more than just a coincidence. It seems like a gentle, yet poignant reminder from God not to worry about what tomorrow holds because we are taken care of—much like the sparrows. And it reassures me that no matter the challenges we face, there is a plan and presence caring for us always.

---

3   Cory Asbury, "Sparrow," written by Cory Asbury and Ethan Hulse, Bethel Music Publishing / Cory Asbury Publishing, 2023, track 2 on Pioneer, Bethel Music, 2023, MP3 audio.

I promise, Eliana, that Mom and I will take good care of you, just as we are being cared for. Whatever the future brings, we'll face it together with love and faith.

CHAPTER TEN

VISIONS AND CONNECTIONS

May 28, 2024

Today marks the beginning of another journey—not just across continents but also into the depths of spirituality and connection. As I settled into the tropical embrace of Liberia, Costa Rica, and then planned for the rapid shifts of Rapid City, South Dakota, I found myself delving into a realm that until now had been more of Mom's domain than mine. The book *Spirit Babies*, which I decided to experience in its audio form, beckoned with promises of understanding and insights into chakras, past lives, and more.

In the solitude of my hotel room, away from the usual bustle, I discovered a peaceful mindset that allowed me to be more receptive. It was as though every question about who you might be and how we could connect spiritually was heightened by this new environment—an openness stirring in my heart.

I've always listened to Mom discuss these topics with a mixture of intrigue and skepticism. Yet, something about today, about this journey, seemed to demand a deeper engagement. The book became a bridge between my guarded skepticism and a budding curiosity about the spiritual connections that might be swirling invisibly around us.

As the narrator's voice unfolded the mysteries of spirit babies and the energy that children can see, I thought back to stories of Colton, who once claimed to see a mysterious figure in our Texas home. The book suggested such sights might be the result of open spiritual channels in children—channels that we, perhaps unknowingly, close off over time. It made me wonder about the layers of reality we are blind to and how much of it you might one day perceive.

The meditation techniques described—one involving rainbow breathing and particularly one which required visualizing a growing green oval and chanting—were entirely new to me. Despite my usual reserve, I found a quiet spot by the pool, under the vast Costa Rican sky, and gave myself over to the practice. With each breath, the vivid, green oval grew, and I envisioned it bursting and merging into me, a conduit for connection with what I hoped might be your guardian angel, Eliana.

I wasn't expecting a dramatic revelation. The author had tempered expectations, suggesting that any response might be subtle, perhaps coming through signs or dreams long after the meditation. Yet, as I sat there, green streaks floated across my closed eyes, coalescing into a vibrant orb. It was unexpected and profound, leaving me to wonder if this was a response from you, a sign of your presence in our lives even now.

Sitting in that tropical setting, I felt the soft breeze on my face and, for the first time, I truly allowed myself to believe that our connection transcends just the medical process. It felt as though God was nudging me, whispering, *"Trust Me in even the unseen places."*

Sitting on my balcony, just moments later, as distant thunder rolled and birds chirped undisturbed, a smile found its way to my face. It wasn't the clear voice or definitive sign I might have imagined, but it was a connection—a feeling of being touched by something beyond the ordinary.

This experience has shifted something within me. It has opened a door I had only previously peeked through, inviting me to consider the possibility of a deeper spiritual connection with you, my future child. As I continue this trip, carrying with me the impressions of today's meditation, I feel a renewed commitment to being there for you, to ensure that you grow up knowing you are deeply loved by your parents. We are preparing ourselves, emotionally and spiritually, to welcome you into a home filled with love, care, and an openness to the wonders that life has to offer.

The more I learn, the more I realize this path to you is not just about science—it's about faith, spirit, and embracing the unknown. With each passing day, I find myself more eager to see the kind of beautiful soul God is weaving inside your tiny being.

I hope that when you read this one day, you will understand how eagerly we anticipated your all the best to come. You are already cherished, Eliana, and every experience I gather, every insight I gain, is part of the foundation we are building for you.

CHAPTER ELEVEN

TEARS OF TRIUMPH—A GLIMPSE OF GRACE

June 7, 2024

I'll never forget the electric thrill that rattled Mom from the moment she woke up. All morning, she hovered anxiously over her phone, its every buzz sending her heart into a frantic dance as she waited for the call from the doctor's office—the call that would finally unveil your gender. Each time the screen lit up, her eyes widened with anticipation, only to dim with disappointment when it was just another work-related interruption. By 10:00 a.m., the tension was a living thing, coiling tighter with every passing minute. I couldn't bear to just sit there—I needed to move, to do something. So, I grabbed the lawnmower and threw myself into the yardwork, the rhythmic hum of the blades a fleeting distraction from the clock ticking toward our 1:15 p.m. appointment at Shady Grove Fertility.

By 12:30 p.m., I completed mowing the front and back yards, my mind split between the neat rows of grass and the looming moment when we'd know. As I finished, wiping sweat from my brow, I stowed the lawnmower and grabbed two cans of soda from the cooler, my hands trembling slightly with nervous energy. That's when I saw her—Mom stepping outside, phone clutched in her hand, her face a mask of something I couldn't decipher. *Was it fear? Joy? Something else entirely?* She looked at me, her voice trembling as she asked, "Can I take a picture of you?"

Clueless, I froze, assuming I must've looked particularly sharp in my black shirt and khaki shorts, the summer sun casting long shadows across the lawn. But then she shifted the phone, and I realized she was recording video. My heart stuttered. *Why now? What was happening?*

Before I could ask, she spoke, her voice breaking with a mixture of awe and disbelief: "All three embryos are girls."

Time stopped. The words hung in the air, fragile and luminous, like the first light of dawn breaking over a dark horizon. My breath caught, a sharp, jagged inhale, and then my eyes—oh, my eyes—filled with tears so suddenly it was as if a dam had burst inside me. "They're all girls?" I whispered, my voice cracking, barely audible over the pounding of my own heart. The chances were so slim—12.5 percent, a whisper of possibility in a sea of uncertainty—and yet here it was, a miracle unfolding before me.

Tears spilled down my cheeks, hot and unstoppable, as I turned to face her fully, my vision blurring with joy. I repeated it again, louder this time, a prayer and a proclamation: "They're all girls?" Each word trembled with disbelief, with gratitude, with a love so vast it threatened to swallow me whole. In that moment, the world fell away—the lawn, the soda cans still clutched in my hands, the hum of distant traffic—and all I could see was Mom, her own eyes glistening, mirroring my tears.

Overcome, I dropped everything, the cans clattering to the ground as I nearly sprinted toward her, closing the distance in three long strides. I pulled her into a hug, our tears mingling, our hearts beating in sync as a wave of relief, gratitude, and raw, unfiltered amazement crashed over us both. It was as if God Himself had reached down, wrapping us in a promise too beautiful to fathom—three healthy, genetically perfect female embryos, each a beacon of hope, each a chance to finally hold our little girl without enduring another cycle of injections, bruises, and pain.

The drive to Shady Grove Fertility was a blur of laughter and tears, our words tumbling over each other as we chattered about which embryo we might choose, our voices thick with excitement. We fought the urge to call family and friends like Amanda or Josh, knowing the clinic would caution us to keep this under wraps until everything was more settled. The secrecy was agonizing, but it was the kind of agony fueled by hope—a hope so bright it lit up the darkest corners of our journey.

From that day on, every shot, every ache, every anxious thought found its anchor in this extraordinary truth. This was one of the sweetest afternoons of our entire IVF journey—the afternoon we discovered that a special glimmer of God's grace had chosen us to be the parents of a little girl, times three. It made the swollen injection sites, the stinging medication, the ocean of tears behind us feel not just worthwhile but sacred. As I sat in the car, wiping away tears of joy, I knew this moment was a gift—not just for us but for anyone who dared to hope that their own miracle was just around the corner.

Eliana, this month has brought its share of challenges and adjustments. Mom and I received some disheartening news recently—her uterine lining might be thinner than ideal, which has led to a shift in our timeline for the embryo transfer. Nurse Nancy and Dr. Timmreck have decided to extend Mom's birth-control regimen for an additional week, followed by a series of tests, pushing our plans from late February to early March. Although this change complicates my vacation scheduling due to bids placed last year, the flexibility of my post-birth benefits reassures us that we can manage these obstacles effectively.

I still remember the pit in my stomach when we found out her uterine lining needed more time. Doubt crept in, whispering, *What if this never goes according to plan?* But I felt God gently reminding me that His timing often looks different from ours—and His is always better.

Despite these hurdles, we remain steadfast in our faith that this is all part of a greater plan. Yesterday, while flying from Los Angeles to Cancun, I immersed myself in two educational videos about the frozen embryo-transfer process, seeking to understand every aspect of what Mom will soon undergo. It's crucial for us to stay informed and prepared for the next steps.

Here's the revised IVF calendar that now guides our journey:

- June 27: Mom takes her last birth control pill.
- June 28: We have a pre-med FET appointment at Shady Grove Fertility for bloodwork and an ultrasound to check the lining.
- June 29: Mom starts taking Estrace medication orally, three times a day.
- July 12: Lining-check appointment. If all looks well, Mom begins daily injections the following day.
- July 13: Daily injections start, continuing until Mom is 10 weeks pregnant.
- July 18: Scheduled for the frozen embryo transfer.

Reading those dates on paper stirred a mix of nerves and excitement in me. Each milestone represented a little step forward, but also another chance for hiccups. Even so, I wrote them down in my planner and took a moment to pray, trusting that God would hold each date in His hands.

On June 28, we visited Shady Grove Fertility for the crucial lining check. The appointment brought us some much-needed good news— the ultrasound showed that everything was perfect with Mom's lining, and she was cleared to start her new medication regimen immediately.

This confirmation keeps us on track for the July 18 embryo transfer, a date we now eagerly anticipate.

The blend of clinical precision and emotional roller coaster that defines this IVF journey is overwhelming at times, but moments of progress like these bolster our spirits tremendously. We're very excited and hopeful about the upcoming transfer, imagining that soon, one of these embryos will become you, our much-longed-for child.

Mom and I are clinging to each piece of positive news, allowing it to fuel our optimism and carry us through the uncertainties still ahead. As we prepare for what we hope will be a successful transfer, our hearts are full of hope, dreams, and a deep desire to finally meet you, Eliana.

I can't count how many nights I've gone to bed whispering thanks, especially for Mom's resilience. She fights so many battles behind the scenes—adjusting medication times, tracking appointments—and does it all with unwavering grace. In each challenge, I see her love for you shining through.

CHAPTER TWELVE

ANTICIPATION AND ADJUSTMENTS

June 12 to July 13, 2024

My dear Eliana, it has been a bustling few weeks filled with joy, challenges, and significant milestones. After a spirited celebration of Dave and Colton's birthdays, your mom and I, along with the rest of the family, ventured to Detroit. There, we immersed ourselves in the warmth of family gatherings, celebrating not just individual birthdays but the collective spirit of togetherness that defines our family. Nana W and Papa, alongside Aunt Nicki and Aunt Jenni, hosted wonderful dinners and cookouts, marking the Fourth of July with festivity and joy.

Between laughter and sparklers, I found myself thinking of the day you would join these family gatherings—one more little spark lighting up our home with the joy only a new child can bring.

During this period, Mom began her prescribed medications as part of our IVF journey. Initially, everything progressed smoothly, but around July 5, she started to experience severe migraines. These migraines were so intense that they disrupted our usual activities; Mom had to miss out on some family fun, seeking solace in quiet and rest. Despite the physical toll, her resilience has been nothing short of inspiring.

Watching her power through debilitating headaches made me appreciate her strength all over again. I'd catch her lying down with a damp cloth over her forehead, but the moment any family member needed her, she'd push herself to be fully present, all while quietly praying for relief.

On a logistical note, we faced some scheduling challenges due to the medication's effects and our travel. Mom was scheduled to start her progesterone in oil (PIO) shots on July 13, an essential step in preparing for the upcoming embryo transfer. Although our trip to Detroit was enriching, it left Mom needing rest, impacting our original plan for her to accompany me on a work trip. Instead, she bravely administered her first PIO shot herself at home, marking the beginning of a daily routine that will continue for the next ten weeks.

Our visit to Shady Grove Fertility on July 11 for an ultrasound and blood work brought us some encouraging news: Mom's uterine lining was still in perfect condition for the embryo transfer. The medical team's go-ahead to start the PIO shots reinforced our hopes and solidified our schedule. The excitement was palpable; everything medical was aligning just as we had hoped.

However, life's penchant for drama didn't miss us. My work schedule poses a potential conflict with the embryo transfer date set for July 18. Determined not to miss this pivotal moment, I am prepared to adjust my work commitments, ensuring I can support Mom and witness the transfer.

Amid these scheduling complications, I prayed often, asking God to carve out the path so I could be by her side when it mattered most. Each day, we held onto hope that all these moving parts—medical, travel, and work—would align for the miracle we'd been seeking.

As we approach this significant event, our hearts are filled with anticipation and a bit of anxiety—normal emotions given the stakes. We're also planning a gender-reveal party for the family back in Michigan, contemplating creative ways to announce your expected arrival. From balloons with hidden messages to color-changing liquids, we're crafting an event that will be as unique as the life we hope to celebrate.

Eliana, each step we take is a step closer to you. As I write these lines, it feels as if I am not just chronicling events but speaking directly to you, across time and space, through the love that already binds us. I will update you soon on how everything unfolds. Until then, know that every decision, every effort, is made with you in mind.

With all the love a heart can hold,

Dad

CHAPTER THIRTEEN

THE BEGINNING OF FOREVER

July 16 to 18, 2024

These past few days have encapsulated a lifetime of emotions, marking a definitive chapter in our journey toward becoming a family of five. On July 16, as I settled into the quiet of my hotel room in San Francisco, preparing for my overnight flight to Pittsburgh, every thought was tethered to what awaited at home. The anticipation of the upcoming embryo transfer for you, Eliana, made every minute away stretch endlessly.

Two days later, on July 18, the morning greeted us not just with a merciful drop in the sweltering temperatures but also with a sense of serene promise. As we left for Shady Grove Fertility, the air was crisp, and the world seemed to pause in respect for the day's potential. As I backed the car out of the driveway, the radio serendipitously played "I Believe" by Phil Wickham.[4] This song, which had underscored the beginning of our IVF journey at the very same artist's concert, now seemed to come full circle, reassuring us of the divine presence in our lives. The moment was so poignant that it brought tears to my eyes, a silent acknowledgment of the significance of the day.

---

4   Phil Wickham, "I Believe."

I couldn't help but whisper a prayer of thanks—thanking God for aligning these simple yet profound moments, reminding us that our faith had carried us to this exact place and time.

We arrived at the clinic and, with each step toward the fourth floor, our hearts beat a symphony of anticipation and nerves. The reception area of Shady Grove was a familiar yet suddenly awe-inspiring setting as we checked in for one of the most significant appointments of our lives. Before the procedure, an email notification drew our attention to what was described as our daughter's first picture — an image of your embryo, magnified and captured beautifully as it was being prepared for transfer. Mom and I, clutching each other's hands, shared a moment of awe and silent prayers in the waiting area.

The procedure was scheduled for 1:00 p.m., but it wasn't until 1:10 p.m. that the doctor came in to explain the process to us, and the weight of the moment settled deeply in my chest. I meticulously set up my camera, determined to capture every detail of the procedure on the screen—this was not just a medical procedure; it was the moment our family would grow.

There's something about watching life begin in such a precise, scientific way that leaves you breathless. Knowing God's hand and modern medicine are working in tandem feels like a small miracle unfolding right before our eyes.

Post-transfer, as we were left alone briefly, the magnitude of our actions felt surreal. I helped Mom as she dressed, stealing a moment to kiss her belly and whisper promises of love to you. It felt as though our lives were both paused and playing at double speed, every second infused with profound significance.

Our next stop was unexpected yet oddly fitting: McDonald's. According to an IVF tradition Mom had read about online, consuming French fries post-transfer was considered good luck. While it seemed whimsical, sitting next to Mom, sharing fries in a quiet corner of McDonald's, I felt a deep peace wash over us. It was a simple, perfect moment of normalcy amidst a journey filled with extraordinary steps.

We ended our day at Moby Dick in Germantown, a favorite little Mediterranean spot where we could dine under the open sky. The evening was beautiful, reflective of our moods: hopeful and celebratory. As we discussed our future and the larger family we were soon to become, our conversation was filled with laughter and dreams.

In the back of my mind, I kept hearing the refrain from "I Believe" replaying softly, like a soundtrack to this monumental day. It reminded me that while we'd fought hard to reach this point, there was a higher hand guiding us all along.

Eliana, today marked a foundational shift in our lives. You are woven into the very fabric of our being now, part of a love story that grows with each passing day. We are a family forever changed, forever grateful, and forever waiting to meet you. Your mom is the embodiment of strength and love—a beacon of what it means to be a devoted parent.

This chapter of our lives, this beginning of forever with you, is a testament to the power of love, faith, and family. One day, I hope you read these words and understand the depth of our joy and the breadth of our commitment to you. We love you, now and always.

With all my heart,

Dad

CHAPTER FOURTEEN

TRIALS AND TRIBULATIONS

July 28, 2024

The last eight days have been a relentless storm of emotions, a rollercoaster ride we couldn't have anticipated. Fresh off the high of what we desperately hoped was a successful embryo transfer, Mom, the boys, and I had planned to escape to Detroit on July 19 for a much-needed break from life's constant pressures. But as it turned out, fate had other plans.

When we woke up on Friday, July 19, we were thrust into chaos—a global Internet outage caused by a third-party antiviral software upgrade. The world as we knew it came to a standstill. The Internet was down everywhere, crippling most airlines. As cancellations rolled in, our dream of a stress-free week in Michigan crumbled before our eyes. The stress we hoped to leave behind only multiplied, morphing into an overwhelming, inescapable reality.

Flights were canceled one after another, and each cancellation felt like a blow to our already fragile hope. The last flight to Detroit became our beacon in the storm, but it too was eventually snuffed out. Amidst the chaos, an opportunity to pick up a lucrative three-day premium-pay trip appeared. It was a tough call, but the financial benefit was too significant to ignore. With a heavy heart and fingers crossed, I hoped that Mom and the boys would somehow make it to Michigan and find a way to relax while I went to work.

Against all odds, Mom and the boys managed to secure seats on an early Saturday morning Delta flight. Relief washed over me as they departed, but my own journey began, filled with trepidation and the weight of our uncertain plans.

On Sunday, in search of clarity and connection, Mom turned to Ann for another tarot card reading, seeking guidance and a deeper bond with you, Eliana. These are the notes she took from her session:

- The first card that Ann pulled had a queen and a skeleton on it with the queen clutching three coins. Ann said, "You have three embryos, don't you?" Mom confirmed, and Ann said the queen holding the three coins represented the three embryos.

- Ann could tell Mom was very stressed and scared. She advised Mom to start making decisions without second-guessing, because she often goes back and forth, wanting someone else to make the decision for her.

- Ann kept seeing new beginnings and emphasized clearing out old energy and bringing in the new.

- The sun card showed two babies, and Ann said that there was gunk and stress taking up space, making Eliana feel like there was no room for her.

- Ann noted the strong male energy in the house and mentioned that Eliana might be different from the boys, who would be confused about how to interact with her.

- Eliana told Ann to reassure Mom that everything would be okay.

- Ann mentioned that Dave would help a lot with Eliana and that he would not feel resentment for helping; he would want to help.

- Eliana was described as an indigo child, similar to Dave, indicating a higher level of spiritual awareness and maturity.

- Ann said Eliana would be busy, kind, patient, and loving, bringing everyone together and teaching Mom many things.

- Colton was predicted to be very jealous, having trouble adjusting and sharing Mom with Eliana.

- The second little boy spirit was at peace, willing to come if chosen, but happy either way.

- Ann noted that Mom's throat chakra was blocked, indicating fear of speaking up and being concerned about the consequences of expressing herself.

- Eliana was implanting, but Mom needed to work on her emotions and stress levels because too much stress could lead to losing the pregnancy.

- Ann advised Mom to stop taking on others' burdens, as it was adding unnecessary weight and heaviness.

As if the previous days hadn't been chaotic enough, my trip home on July 22 turned into a nightmare. Multiple storms delayed my return, and I found myself in Baltimore at 1:30 a.m., sleeping in a makeshift crew room on a terribly uncomfortable chair. My plan to catch a 6 a.m. flight to Detroit was thwarted by yet another cancellation, with Delta still reeling from the outage. Determined to reunite with my family, I drove to Washington Dulles, desperate to get on the first flight to Detroit.

The drive felt interminable, but, finally, I was back in Michigan. After a wonderful few days with our family we began to prepare for out flight back to Maryland. However, our return flights were fully booked. Just as hope seemed to dim, a last-minute check revealed six open seats. In a flurry of action, Mom and I scrambled to gather the boys' belongings, rushing to the airport and miraculously making it onto the flight home Tuesday night. Relief washed over us as we touched down, exhausted but together.

At home, we sought solace in familiar comforts. Thursday brought a much-needed distraction. I took the boys to see *Twister* in 4DX—a sensory adventure with moving seats, wind, and rain effects. Colton and Dave were enthralled, and for a few hours, the chaos melted away, giving Mom a peaceful day to herself.

But our reprieve was short-lived. Friday dawned with new challenges. Mom's dad—whom I affectionately call Papito—awoke in excruciating pain, and for the first time we learned he'd taken a bad fall a few days earlier. It was a crushing revelation, and Mom, ever the dutiful daughter, persuaded him to go to the hospital. She spent an extraordinarily long and stressful day by his side, watching him endure broken ribs while also racing the clock to get home for her crucial progesterone shot. By God's grace, Papito was discharged just in time for her to make it back and administer it.

Eliana, the vacation that was supposed to be our oasis turned into one of the most stressful periods we've faced. Ann's warnings echo in our minds: Too much stress could jeopardize your journey to us. We need you more than ever. Mom is scared, and we are holding on to faith, believing in your strength and resilience. Eight days post-embryo transfer, we pray fervently for you to attach and grow strong. We need you, Eliana, and we are eagerly awaiting the day we can finally meet you.

Through every canceled flight, every tough conversation, and every exhausting moment, I found myself silently whispering: "God, please pave the way. We can't do this without You." Sometimes it felt like we were on the brink of losing hope, but our faith kept pulling us back, reminding us that a miracle only takes one 'yes' from Him.

With all our love,

Dad

CHAPTER FIFTEEN

A STORM OF EMOTIONS AND A RAY OF HOPE

August 15, 2024

The last few weeks have felt like a relentless storm—waves of grief, fear, hope, and love crashing over us, each one threatening to pull us under. Yet, through it all, Mom has been nothing short of a warrior, her strength and resilience shining as a beacon for us all, especially for you, Eliana. This chapter of our lives has been one of the most challenging yet, but it's also been a testament to the unbreakable bond of family and the incredible strength of your mom.

It all began on Friday, July 26. Mom took Papito to the hospital after hearing him in pain, only to discover that he had a broken rib from a fall he hadn't told her about and that his cancer had metastasized into his bones. The diagnosis was crushing, a heavy blow that none of us were prepared for. Yet, as the doctors spoke in their clinical terms, Mom stood strong, absorbing the news with a quiet resolve. She knew this was just the beginning of a long, painful journey, but she was determined to be there for Papito, to carry him through this dark tunnel with the same unwavering love she has always shown.

Then, just a few days later, on Monday, July 29, the storm grew darker. Mom woke up to find her own mother, whom we also call Nana (she is Nana M), had suffered a mini-stroke in the middle of the night. Once again, Mom was thrust into the role of caregiver, rushing her mom to the hospital. It was a terrifying experience—seeing her mother, the woman who had always been her pillar of strength, suddenly so vulnerable. Yet, Mom didn't flinch. She was scared, but she didn't let it show. She knew she had to be strong, not just for her mother but also for you, Eliana. She was carrying you through all of this, every moment of fear and doubt tempered by the hope that you were growing stronger inside her.

The following day, July 30, the storm hit again. Mom heard Papito screaming from the basement and rushed to his side. He was in agony; he had fallen out of bed, and the pain was unbearable. She called 911 and, within minutes, an ambulance arrived to take him to Holy Cross Hospital. In the chaos, Mom had to cancel her bloodwork appointment at Shady Grove Fertility for the second day in a row. As she watched the ambulance speed away, sirens blaring, she felt the weight of the world on her shoulders. But she didn't falter. She knew she had to be there for Papito, no matter what.

The next day, July 31, was another grueling test of Mom's strength. She spent the entire day at the hospital, waiting for news from hospice, all while trying to find a moment to focus on you, Eliana. Despite the overwhelming fear and sadness, there was finally a glimmer of hope. Mom made it to Shady Grove Fertility that morning, where they took her blood to see if she was pregnant. That afternoon, a small ray of sunshine broke through the clouds—her HCG levels came back at 938. Anything over 100 is good, and this number was a strong indicator that you were there, growing inside her. It was a moment of pure joy amidst the sea of sorrow, a reminder that even in the darkest times, life finds a way.

August 2 brought more whirlwind emotions as Papito was transferred to a hospice facility. The weight of what was coming was heavy on all our hearts, but there was a small comfort in knowing that he was finally comfortable. The doctor told us that Papito was in better shape than we had anticipated, and that brought a big smile to Mom's face, a brief but precious relief in a week that had been filled with nothing but worry and pain. On August 1, Mom had gone for her second round of bloodwork, and the results were just as promising. Her HCG levels had doubled to 1,945—another sign that you were holding on, that you were as strong as your mom. As of August 2, Mom was five weeks pregnant, and the chances of miscarriage had dropped to 7 percent. In one life we were facing an end, but in another we were witnessing a beautiful beginning.

But the balance of life and death is never simple. Three days before Papito passed, Mom whispered to him through tears that you were on the way—a baby girl, no less—and that your middle name would be José María, carrying his name forward. Even in his weakened state, Papito gathered the last ounces of his strength to open his eyes. "Really?" he murmured, the love and surprise evident in his voice. It was a fleeting moment of pure emotional connection between a father and his daughter, one that would stay with Mom forever. In that instant, all the sadness parted like a curtain, revealing the depth of their bond—a bond so powerful that Papito's eyes shone one last time, satisfied by the knowledge that his legacy would live on in you.

On August 6, exactly one year to the day that Grandma Frost passed away, we were awakened abruptly at 4:40 a.m. by a call we had both been dreading: Papito had passed. We rushed to the Casey House hospice facility to be by his side. When we arrived, his body was still warm, draped with a white sheet. Mom and her sister Laura spent the next five hours with him, holding his hand, sharing stories, and reminiscing about the life of a man who had lived with such love and vitality.

Your middle name, José María, carries the weight of a man who cherished his daughter so deeply that, in a way, it felt as though he departed this world to make room for you. Eliana, you are a gift from God, sent from heaven wrapped in Papito's love—a testament to the resilience and devotion that connects generations. Even in farewell, he left behind an inheritance of unwavering affection, which we now pass on to you.

Jose Maria Ricardo de Cores Risso was born on September 13, 1945, in Uruguay. He was a man of many colors and talents—full of jokes, charisma, and charm. His life was a tapestry woven with rich experiences, from his travels around the world to the deep love he had for his family. Saying goodbye was the hardest thing we've ever had to do, but it was also a moment of profound reflection on the legacy he left behind—a legacy of love, strength, and resilience that we hope to carry forward, especially as we prepare to welcome you into this world, Eliana.

The days that followed were a blur of grief and adjustment. August 13 and August 14 passed in a haze of sorrow and preparation. Mom was trying to find a new rhythm without Papito, while also dealing with the physical toll of early pregnancy. She was often nauseous, and for a few days she ran a low-grade fever, a sign that her body was working overtime to nurture you. But even in the midst of her grief and physical discomfort, Mom never lost sight of the miracle growing inside her.

As we prepared for our family vacation to Atlantis in Nassau, there was a palpable sense of anticipation—an eagerness to escape the trials of life, if only for a few days. But before we could leave, Mom had one more visit to Shady Grove Fertility. On August 14, we received the confirmation we had been hoping for: Mom was officially six weeks, four days pregnant, and your due date, just as Ann predicted, was set for April 5, 2025. We saw your tiny little heart beating at 120 beats per minute on the ultrasound screen, and it was the most beautiful sight we've ever seen.

In that moment, everything else faded away. The grief, the stress, the fear—all of it melted as we watched your little head, your little tail, and your heart beating so rapidly. It was a moment that will stay with us forever, a memory we will cherish for the rest of our lives. We captured a video and a photo of the ultrasound, and I know that these images will be a source of joy and comfort for years to come. It might sound silly, but I already knew I loved you and seeing that tiny image of you made me fall in love with you even more.

Mom and I are so incredibly excited to watch you grow, to continue on this journey with you, and to begin a new chapter in our lives. The days that have passed have been dark and difficult, but they have also been filled with moments of light and love. And as we move forward, we do so with hope in our hearts and with the unwavering belief that you, Eliana, are a warrior, just like your mom.

In each tear shed for Papito, I could sense an echo of love that would one day blossom in your heart. Even as we mourned, we rejoiced in the stirrings of new life—proof that darkness never has the final word when faith stands guard at the door.

With all our love,

Dad

CHAPTER SIXTEEN

OUR FIRST VACATION AS A FAMILY OF FIVE

September 3, 2024

Eliana, your first vacation might be just a distant memory for you now, but for us, it was unforgettable. It was August 17, 2024, when we left Washington, DC, and flew to Nassau in the Bahamas for a week of family fun at the iconic Atlantis Resort. This wasn't just any trip; it was our first vacation knowing we were a family of five. Mom and I couldn't stop talking about how surreal it felt to know you were with us, even though you were still growing inside her.

We stayed at The Royal, which truly lived up to its name. The grandeur of the resort was unlike anything we had ever seen. The lobby felt like a palace—marble floors, high ceilings, and intricate chandeliers that sparkled like the ocean. The view from our room was breathtaking. When we looked out over the balcony, we saw the deep turquoise ocean stretching as far as the eye could see, its waves crashing softly on the shore. At night, the lights of Atlantis twinkled below, casting a magical glow over the resort. Even the air was different—warm, salty, and full of excitement.

But the real adventure began at Aquaventure, the massive waterpark that felt like a playground for both kids and adults. The boys could hardly contain their excitement. We started with the smaller water slides, easing into the day, but it wasn't long before they were begging to take on the Leap of Faith. Just looking up at the towering Mayan Temple made my heart race, but there was no backing out. The slide was practically vertical, dropping you straight down through a clear tube surrounded by sharks. I could hear the boys screaming as they took the plunge, their voices full of thrill and terror at the same time. I went down last, the adrenaline pumping through my veins as I shot through the tunnel, water rushing all around me. It was terrifying and exhilarating all at once—definitely one for the memory books.

And then, of course, there was the ocean. The Bahamian waters were as stunning as they looked in postcards—vivid shades of blue and green, shimmering under the sun. But they weren't as peaceful as they appeared. The waves were fierce that week, crashing onto the shore with surprising force. Twice, the ocean took my sunglasses, and both times I thought, *Well, there goes another pair!* But even as the waves knocked us around, we couldn't help but dive back in, laughing every time we were sent tumbling.

I found myself looking over at Mom every now and then, her belly beginning to show the slightest hint of you. She'd rest her hand protectively there, a soft smile on her lips that spoke volumes about her gratitude and excitement.

When we needed a break from the thrill, we would head over to the Lazy River, where time seemed to slow down. Floating under the tropical sun, with nothing but the sound of water gently rippling by, I found myself thinking about how blessed we were to be together, to have this time with you even though you hadn't yet entered the world. Mom was lying on a tube next to me, and I could see the exhaustion on her face, but also her contentment. She wasn't feeling great, and the trip was wearing her out, but she never complained. Instead, she smiled as she watched the boys splash and play, soaking in every moment with us.

Mom and I had our own quiet celebration while at Atlantis—it was our second wedding anniversary. It wasn't the typical romantic dinner and sunset stroll, but it was perfect in its own way. We shared laughs, reminisced about the past couple of years, and even though we were in the middle of a bustling resort, we found time to reflect on everything we'd been through and what lay ahead. I marveled at how she managed everything—especially the daily progesterone shots she needed to keep the pregnancy healthy. Every day at 7 p.m., without fail, we had to find a spot to give her the injection. We got creative—one time, it was in the men's bathroom in the hotel basement, another time, in a phone booth at a different part of the resort. It wasn't glamorous, but it was part of our routine and, somehow, it felt like a small victory every time we got it done.

One of the most special moments of the trip was taking our first photo as a family of five. We stood in front of The Royal, the sun setting behind us, casting a golden glow over everything. The boys were still buzzing from the day's adventures, and though you weren't physically in the picture, you were very much part of it. I couldn't stop smiling, knowing that this was just the first of many family photos with you.

The food at Atlantis wasn't exactly five-star, but it didn't matter. We were too busy making memories. Every meal, every snack—even the not-so-great ones—became part of the story of our first big adventure as a family.

But as the days passed, we began to feel the pull to get back home. We had an important appointment waiting for us on August 23—another ultrasound to check on you, and it felt like time was standing still as we counted down the hours. That day finally arrived, and at 1 p.m., we found ourselves sitting in the exam room, anxiously waiting for the doctor to come in.

There you were, eight millimeters long—our little raspberry. We watched in awe as your tiny heart fluttered on the screen, beating at 164 beats per minute. It was a beautiful sight, one that filled both Mom and me with so much joy and relief. You were thriving, and we could see it right there on the monitor. The doctor told us you were a day ahead of schedule, which made us smile—already proving to be strong and determined, just like your mom. We left the office with ultrasound pictures in hand, and the first thing Mom did when we got home was put one of them into a special frame, just for you.

Every flicker of your heartbeat seemed to mirror our own relief and awe. In that sterile exam room, I felt God's gentle whisper: "Here is the miracle you prayed for."

With that appointment, Mom's journey with Shady Grove Fertility officially came to an end. Her transfer was a complete success, and now we were moving into the next chapter of this incredible journey. Mom's first appointment at Capital Women's Care was scheduled for August 27, and we were excited to get another look at you.

The past few months hadn't been easy, especially for Mom. She had endured more than ninety progesterone shots, each one more painful than the last, but she never gave up. She pushed through the discomfort, the exhaustion, the bruises, because she knew that every shot, every moment of pain, was bringing us one step closer to meeting you. Her strength is something I'll never stop admiring, and I know that you, Eliana, will have that same strength in you.

By the end of August, Mom was down to her final four shots, and the relief was palpable. She couldn't wait to be done with them, to finally move past that phase of the process. Her body was sore and she was tired beyond words, but she kept going. She kept fighting, because that's what a warrior does.

As we moved into September, the boys returned to school—fifth grade for Dave and seventh grade for Colton. It hit me then that this would be our last summer, our last holidays, as a family of four.

The next time we celebrated, you would be with us. The thought filled my heart with so much anticipation and love. Our journey as a family of five had already begun, and we couldn't wait to share the next chapter with you.

There's a part of me that will never forget this season—how we balanced the sweetness of a growing family with the harsh reality of daily injections. Yet, every struggle made each victory sweeter, and every day reaffirmed our faith. I tucked away each memory, each answered prayer, hoping you'd one day understand just how cherished you truly are.

With all my love,

Dad

CHAPTER SEVENTEEN

HELLO, LITTLE ONE

September 05, 2024

Hi Eliana,

Today marks a big milestone—Mom and I have officially reached Week 10 of your incredible journey! At this point, you're about the size of a strawberry, growing so fast and making us more excited every day. Each week, we marvel at the little changes that make you more and more real to us. This week, we learned that your little arms and legs are beginning to take shape, and your tiny fingers and toes are no longer webbed—you're already becoming your own person!

Your heart is beating strong, pumping blood through your growing body, and your organs are working hard, developing for the future. It's truly awe-inspiring to think about everything happening inside Mom's belly. In just a few weeks, we'll be able to see you in even more detail during your next ultrasound. We can't wait for that moment—every little change feels like a step closer to holding you in our arms.

We spend a lot of time imagining what you'll be like. Will you have Mom's eyes? My smile? We talk about you every day, wondering what your little personality will be, how you'll laugh, and how you'll fill our home with your presence. The joy and anticipation are hard to put into words—it's like we're already in love with someone we haven't met yet.

This past week, Mom and I have been focusing on keeping everything calm and stress-free. We want to make sure that you feel surrounded by love, peace, and safety. Mom has been feeling a whirlwind of emotions, but she's staying strong for you. It's incredible how much strength she's shown throughout this process. She's doing everything she can to keep you healthy and happy, and we're doing our best to make sure she's comfortable and supported.

I find myself praying more often than usual—asking God to guard your tiny heart, your delicate bones, and the bright spirit I know is already forming. It's like each prayer weaves another protective layer of faith around you and your mom.

We've also been praying for you every night. We imagine the day we'll finally meet you—your tiny fingers wrapped around ours, the softness of your little cheeks, and that first kiss on your forehead. We feel so blessed to be on this journey with you, and even though you're not here yet, you're already such a huge part of our lives.

Mom has just a few more shots left now, and we're counting down the days until she can finally stop. It's been a tough road, especially for her, but every step brings us closer to you. You've got one amazing mom, and we know you're going to grow up to be just as strong and resilient as she is.

Keep growing, little girl. We love you more than you could ever know, and we can't wait to see the beautiful person you're becoming.

With all my love,

Dad

CHAPTER EIGHTEEN

GROWING TOGETHER

September 18, 2024

Hi Eliana,

This week, you're eleven weeks along, and you've grown so much! According to the Bump app, you're now about the size of a lime, around 1.6 inches long, and weighing about a quarter of an ounce. You're starting to move around, even though we can't feel it just yet. You're developing tiny tooth buds, and your little diaphragm is forming, which means that soon you'll be able to hiccup! All of your vital organs are in place and beginning to function, preparing you for life outside the womb. It's incredible to think about how much you're growing every single day.

But you know, sweet girl, you're not the only one growing during this pregnancy. As Mom and I prepare for your arrival, we're learning more about ourselves and about each other. It's not always easy—being married, expecting a baby, managing a household, and raising two boys. We've had moments of disagreement and frustration, times when the stress and exhaustion bubble over, and we say things we don't mean or act out of emotion rather than love.

I wish I could snap my fingers and be the perfect dad, the perfect husband, but life doesn't work that way. Each conflict, each misunderstanding, is another chance to learn grace. And maybe that's part of God's plan: Teaching us how to be better people so we can become the parents you deserve.

It's not just you who's developing—Mom and I are growing too, both mentally and emotionally. We've had to learn about the importance of communication, how to handle our emotions, and how to be patient with each other. You see, Mom and I don't fight very often, but when we do, it's usually because we've let too much build up. I tend to keep things inside, and so does Mom. But when we bottle things up, eventually, the pot boils over. We end up hurting each other's feelings, even though that's never our intention.

I've learned that I need to communicate better. I can't keep running away from my issues or pretending that everything's fine when it's not. And I've also had to remind myself that Mom is going through an incredible transformation during this pregnancy. Her body is changing, her hormones are fluctuating, and she's working ten times harder than normal to keep you healthy. Sometimes, that makes things more difficult for both of us. But that's part of the process—learning how to support each other through the challenges and still show love and patience.

The other day, I wrote your mom an email to express how I've been feeling. We don't always get the chance to talk about everything, and I realized that I've been holding in a lot for a long time. It's not easy admitting when we're struggling, but it's important to be honest about it. I told Mom that even though I've tried to bring up concerns, sometimes it feels like my feelings are dismissed. It's hard, especially when I feel like I'm not seen as a father figure in our blended family. But just like you're growing inside her, we're growing as parents and partners.

Mom and I are still figuring it out—how to build this family, how to communicate better, how to not let things fester. But you should know, in a joking way, don't worry—we aren't going to get divorced! We love each other deeply, and this journey is just one more chapter in our growth as a couple. You're teaching us so much already, even before you're born. We're learning to be more open, more vulnerable, and more forgiving. I pray that, as we raise you, we teach you the importance of keeping an open heart and mind, of talking about what's on your mind instead of letting it weigh you down.

I hope you don't have to learn the lessons I'm still learning at forty-two years old. You deserve to grow up in a home where communication is encouraged, and where love and understanding are at the center of everything. That's what we're working toward, every single day.

So, as you grow physically—your tiny body becoming stronger, your little heart pumping away—we're growing too. We're learning to be better for you, to be the kind of parents you deserve. I promise you that Mom and I are doing everything we can to make sure that, by the time you arrive, we've grown in ways that will allow us to give you the most loving, supportive family you could ever ask for.

Sometimes, I catch myself envisioning the day you're old enough to read these words. I hope you'll see our struggles not as flaws but as evidence of two people committed to becoming the parents God intended us to be for you.

Keep growing strong, little one. We love you more than you'll ever know.

Love you,

Dad

CHAPTER NINETEEN

TWELVE WEEKS AND OUR BIG REVEAL

September 21, 2024

Good morning, Eliana! Today, September 21, 2024, you're officially twelve weeks along, and you've hit an exciting milestone in your growth! According to the Bump app, you're now about the size of a plum—around 2.1 inches long and weighing nearly half an ounce. This week, your reflexes are developing, meaning that if we could reach out and touch you, you'd respond by curling your little fingers or flexing your toes. Your tiny facial features are becoming more defined, and your eyelids are fully formed, though still fused shut. Your brain is growing at an astonishing rate, and you've even started developing taste buds. You're making big moves in there, little one!

It's been a busy couple of weeks for both Mom and me. I've been flying and working hard, while Mom has been home, doing the most important work of all—making you! Despite the craziness, we've been pouring our energy into planning a very special event: Your gender-reveal party.

Now, you already know what we know—it's going to be pink! But no one else knows yet, and we can't wait to share it with your Nana W,

Papa, Aunt Nicki, Aunt Jenni, your Godparents Josh and Sarah, and all your cousins. We've got a plan we're pretty excited about.

I admit it: Part of me felt silly going all out for a gender reveal. But then I remembered all the heartbreak, the longing, and the faith that brought us to this point. Why not celebrate you with every ounce of joy we have?

Let me tell you how we've pulled it all together.

Mom and I have ordered a beautiful cherry chip cake with dripped pink ice frosting. The cake topper says it all, but the big surprise is inside. When we cut into it, pink and white M&M candies will come pouring out of the middle—M&Ms with your name on them, announcing to everyone that it's a girl! Some of them even say "Arrival April 2025," which makes it feel so real. The thought of seeing those M&Ms spill out fills me with so much joy—I can already picture everyone's faces when they realize you're a little girl.

That cake, though . . . if you ask your mom, the part she's usually most excited about would be the cake—except that right now, she can't stand cake! Pregnancy has thrown her taste buds for a loop. So, even though she's normally a cake lover, this time she'll be skipping out on that part of the celebration.

The reveal itself? Well, we've got a twist in store. Before we gather everyone to celebrate with the cake, we'll head to Nana W's backyard, where Mom will be holding a big black balloon filled with blue confetti. The balloon will say, "Is it a Boy or Girl?" and everyone will think we're about to pop the balloon for the big reveal, expecting the confetti to announce your gender. But that's where the fun begins.

In true Mom fashion, she'll have a pregnancy moment and *accidentally* let go of the balloon, sending it floating up into the sky. Everyone will be watching it disappear, thinking the reveal has gone wrong. But we've planned for your godfather, Josh, to be flying a drone, and attached to its skids will be one pink and one blue smoke bomb. The drone will fly in dramatically, releasing pink and blue smoke to keep everyone guessing.

While all eyes are on the drone, I'll secretly light four pink smoke bombs hidden in my back pocket. As the drone soars above, I'll set the bombs on the ground and, just when the excitement is at its peak, we'll draw everyone's attention back to us—and all they'll see is pink smoke swirling around Mom, the boys, and me. It's going to be such a thrilling moment!

Unlike with the boys, where we never had the chance for a gender reveal, this time—after everything we've endured just to have you—it felt not just right but essential to make a memory we'd treasure forever. It's like throwing open the windows and letting the world in on our joy, letting them witness how God has breathed life into our greatest hope. For us, this is all new and thrilling, a departure from the past; Millennials didn't really start these big celebrations until after the babies were born, but you, Eliana, you're part of a new era where we turn everything into a party—from gender reveals to celebrating something as simple as a good hair day! Thanks to the generation before you, we're embracing this moment with all the excitement it deserves, making it a sparkling, unforgettable milestone in our journey.

But no matter how silly or dramatic the reveal might seem, it's all for you, Eliana. We're overjoyed to celebrate this moment, to share it with our family, and to let the world know that you, our little girl, are on the way.

This week has been a little stressful with everything going on. I flew back to Michigan to drop off the M&Ms at So Delish, the bakery, and to pick up the smoke bombs from Papa's house, and then I had to get them over to Josh. But it's all been worth it, knowing that in just a few days, we'll have this incredible moment to share with everyone.

On September 26, Mom and I also have an appointment to see your ultrasound again. I can't even describe how much love fills my heart every time we see you growing. Just thinking about it makes me emotional. We've made it through the first trimester, which is always the most stressful part of pregnancy, and although we're not completely in the clear, we've passed a huge milestone.

It's hard to believe that we're already one-third of the way through this journey. In just twenty-eight more weeks, I'll be holding you in my arms, and I couldn't be more excited for that moment. You've already brought so much love into our lives, and I can't wait to meet you and start this new chapter together as a family.

Keep growing strong, my little strawberry. We love you more than you'll ever know.

With all my love,

Dad

CHAPTER TWENTY

STUBBORN LITTLE KICKS

September 26, 2024

Well, Eliana—or should I say my stubborn little kangaroo—today is September 26, 2024, and Mom went for her twelve-week ultrasound. Everything went beautifully. You were nestled in, face down, and we could clearly see the back of your head, your developing spinal cord, and even the progress of your brain. It was a truly amazing experience.

I still can't get over how each ultrasound reveals more of the tiny miracle taking shape inside Mom's belly. Every time I see your outline on that screen, my heart swells with both awe and relief.

We got a bit of a laugh out of your little antics. When the ultrasound tech moved her wand to get a better view of you, she must've pressed somewhere you didn't like because you gave these big, unmistakable kicks! We saw your legs stretch out as if you were saying, *"Hey! I'm busy here!"* Mom giggled and asked if you'd just kicked, even though she couldn't feel it. But we all definitely saw it, and we shared a laugh. I felt a small tear build up in my eye—why, I'm not quite sure. Maybe it was the magic of seeing you move, that little kick showing us your growing strength and personality. It was enough to melt my heart. Through everything we've been through—from joyful days at water parks to the heartache of losing Papito—you are growing strong and already showing us who you are.

Mom came prepared with a list of questions for the doctor, mostly about how she's been feeling. She's twelve-and-a-half weeks into this pregnancy and still dealing with nausea, heartburn, and trouble breathing. The doctor reassured us that the nausea should ease up in a few weeks, and for the heartburn, she recommended an over-the-counter medication called Prilosec. The breathing issue, it turns out, is because you're getting bigger inside Mom, and that growth is pushing her organs around, making her rib cage expand. But out of an abundance of caution, the doctor referred Mom to a cardiologist just to be extra safe.

Mom also did some blood work to verify your blood type and run another round of genetic testing to make sure you're growing healthy and strong. Even though we've already done testing before, we want to be as sure as possible that you're a healthy little girl. It's all part of making sure you have the best possible start to life.

The doctor also handed Mom a bunch of paperwork to review, including details about labor options—whether to try for a natural birth or plan for a cesarean section. Up until today, Mom and I had been leaning toward a natural birth. She remembers how tough her recovery was after Dave's C-section, and she thought maybe natural labor would be a better experience. But after talking to the doctor and recounting Dave's birth story—how she labored all night and then had to go through a C-section anyway—she's now leaning more toward another C-section. Ultimately, it's her choice, and whatever decision she makes will be the best one for you both.

It's a dark, rainy fall day here in Maryland, and we're getting ready to head to Michigan for your big gender reveal this weekend. Both of us are filled with excitement and relief at knowing you're doing so well. Mom has already scheduled her follow-up appointments—another check-up on October 20, and a detailed ultrasound to look at your full anatomy at the twenty-week point on November 20.

Sometimes, as the rain taps against the window, I think about the nights we spent praying for you—wondering if these days would ever come. And here you are, flipping and kicking on screen, reminding us that miracles happen in the most beautiful ways.

So, little one, even as you stretch and kick, reminding us you're growing stronger every day, we're here on the outside getting everything ready for you. We can't wait for the next milestones and all the beautiful moments we have ahead.

With love,

Dad

CHAPTER TWENTY-ONE

THE BIG REVEAL AND A STORMY SURPRISE

September 29, 2024

Week thirteen has arrived, and with it, the day we've been anxiously awaiting—your gender reveal! Today, on September 29, 2024, family and friends gathered in Michigan to celebrate you, Eliana, but of course, no special day in the Wheeler family is without its twists, and this time, the remnants of Hurricane Helene decided to add their own brand of drama to the occasion.

It's funny how we plan and prepare for a perfect moment, yet life often reminds us who's really in control. Even as the winds picked up and the rain pattered, I felt a strange peace. The big day was here, and God knew exactly how it would all unfold.

The morning began calmly enough. Mom and Nana W spent hours in the kitchen, carefully preparing sweet treats for your big reveal: chocolate-covered pretzels, strawberries, Nutter Butter cookies, and a few other delicious surprises. I tried to help out, but my obsessive attention to detail was driving Mom and Nana W crazy—so I decided to be more useful elsewhere and ran some errands. I stopped at the grocery store, picking up some last-minute items: a quart of strawberries and a case of water—$20! I couldn't believe the price for just two items, but I wasn't about to let that get to me. Afterward,

I headed to Party City to pick up the giant black balloon that we'd be using for the reveal. On the way, I stopped by the bakery and picked up the most amazing cake I'd ever seen. It was a work of art, with pink dripped frosting, and hidden inside were pink-and-white M&Ms that held a secret—your name and a special message, waiting to be revealed.

Back at Nana W's house, the decorating frenzy began. Pink and blue balloons filled the space, and we placed tiny ones inside transparent boxes to add to the mystery. Nana W had special lighting in the family room—one lamp glowing pink, the other blue—helping set the stage for the reveal. It was all coming together, but one thing loomed over our heads: the weather. Remnants of Hurricane Helene had been hovering over Michigan all day, and the rain just wouldn't let up. Mom and I felt the weight of it, knowing that the drone and the smoke bombs were crucial to making the reveal as magical as we'd planned. We prayed for a small break in the rain, even just a five-minute window. I quietly asked Papito for a little help from above.

By 4:00 p.m., our guests started to arrive. My Aunt Pam, Aunt Nicki, your cousin Kate, Papa and Grammy Barb, all came with their families. Your godparents, Josh and Sarah came too, bringing their kids along for the celebration. The house was filled with laughter, excitement, and lots of guesses about whether you would be a boy or a girl. Mom and I even opened a few gifts from family, which only added to the energy in the room. Your brothers, Colton and Dave, were rock solid—they didn't give away a thing, even though some of our guests tried their best to pry the secret out of them. I couldn't have been prouder of how strong they were in keeping our surprise.

Around 5:25 p.m., Papa and I headed out to pick up the food. We ordered from BJ's Brewhouse: Parmesan-crusted lemon chicken, beef tri-tip, Caesar salad, and some sides. We also stopped at Jimmy John's for a party pack of subs. When we returned, the house was buzzing with excitement as everyone started filling their plates. But inside me, the pressure was building—I kept checking the weather radar, praying that our break in the rain would come. Josh and I snuck outside a few times, game-planning the drone's flight and mapping out where the smoke bombs would be placed. We thought the best time to do the reveal would be around 7:20 p.m., but God and maybe Papito had other plans.

At 6:45, the skies suddenly opened up, giving us a brief reprieve. I knew right away that this was our moment, and we had to act fast before the rain returned. I rushed into the garage to set up the smoke bombs, signaling Josh to get his drone into position. This was it—our window. I took a deep breath and went inside to gather everyone for the reveal.

With everyone gathered in Nana W's backyard, the anticipation was intense. All eyes were on Mom, who held the black balloon in her hands, ready to reveal whether we were having a boy or a girl. "Three . . . two . . . one . . ." The countdown began. In classic fashion, Mom *accidentally* let the balloon slip from her hands, and it floated up into the sky. I dramatically shouted, "Sasha! What are you doing?" The confusion spread through the crowd as they watched the balloon disappear into the clouds, thinking our big reveal had gone wrong.

My heart was pounding like a drum solo in my chest, but seeing the startled and amused faces reminded me why we'd planned this elaborate surprise: To share a moment of pure, unfiltered joy.

But just as planned, Josh's drone flew into view, trailing both pink and blue smoke. Everyone was watching the drone, trying to figure out what was happening. The suspense was building, and then I made my move. I pulled the pins on the four pink smoke bombs I had hidden and set them on the ground. Suddenly, the backyard filled with clouds of pink smoke.

At first, there was chaos. "Is it twins?" someone yelled, followed by more confusion. But then it dawned on everyone—the smoke was pink. You, our sweet baby girl, were soon going to make your grand entrance into the world. The cheers erupted, and tears filled the eyes of our family and friends. Nana W was the first to run over, wrapping us in a tight hug. Papa hugged me next, his voice shaking with emotion. This moment—the one we had all been waiting for—was finally here, and it was perfect.

Inside, as the excitement began to settle, everyone wanted to know: "What's her name?" That's when we brought out the cake. I carefully cut into it, and as the M&Ms spilled onto the counter, everyone crowded around to read what they said.

"Eliana," they whispered.

"Arrival April 2025. It's a girl."

There was some confusion over the pronunciation at first, so I proudly explained, "It's Eliana, which means 'God has answered' in Hebrew." Aunt Pam and Nana W both burst into tears, realizing the significance of your name. You were named after Papito, just two months after he had passed. Mom had shared with him just days before his passing that you would carry his name, and now, it was official. It was a special, intimate moment—one that we will cherish forever.

That night, as we celebrated your gender reveal, you were thirteen weeks old. According to the Bump, you were about the size of a lemon, roughly three inches long. Your vocal cords were developing, and your bones were beginning to harden. It's incredible to think that, as you grow, you're preparing to join our family—a family already so full of love for you.

The next big step is Mom's twenty-week sonogram, where we'll get to see even more of you. I can't wait for that moment, Eliana. You've already brought so much love and joy into our lives, and I'm counting down the days until I can hold you in my arms. You're a strong little warrior, and I'm so proud to be your dad.

As the night wound down, I caught Mom's eye from across the room. In that moment, we both knew: This day, this celebration, and every swirling cloud of pink smoke were a testimony to how fervently we believe. In God's promises, in our love for each other, and in the amazing future that awaits you, our precious girl.

Love always,

Dad

CHAPTER TWENTY-TWO

WARRIOR MOM AND OUR GROWING PEACH

October 05, 2024

Hello, my beautiful Eliana!

Today is Saturday, October 5, 2024, and it marks a very special milestone—you are now fourteen weeks along! While we can't quite call this a *birthday* since you're still growing in Mom's belly, we'll call it your Conception Day anniversary, or maybe Growth Day. Whatever we choose, it's an amazing milestone as you continue developing into the beautiful little girl we are all waiting to meet.

So, where are you in this incredible journey? At fourteen weeks, you're about the size of a peach, roughly 3.4 inches long, and you weigh around one-and-a-half ounces. Your body is making some big strides this week! You've got those tiny little arms and legs moving now, and although Mom can't feel it yet, you're wiggling around in there! Your facial expressions are developing too, which means you might already be practicing your adorable smiles. Your kidneys are working hard, producing urine and, believe it or not, you're starting to grow some hair! It won't be long until we find out if you'll have a full head of hair like I did as a baby or if you'll come into the world with a cute little bald head like your brothers. Although, let me tell you, with your mom's thick, dark hair, there's no doubt you're coming into this world with a full head of hair—maybe even a little ponytail or braid!

This week, your mom is noticing some changes too. According to Bump, at fourteen weeks, the top of her uterus is starting to shift higher up in her abdomen, which is making things a bit uncomfortable for her at times. She's got some heartburn, her taste buds are all over the place, and she's feeling nauseous more often than not, but she's handling it all like the absolute warrior she is. Mom's body is in full transformation mode, making room for you, and though it's not always easy, she's got that mom strength flowing through her.

Despite the aches and unpredictability, she keeps on smiling. Every day, I see her press a hand to her belly, her eyes lighting up with gratitude for this gift of life—and in those moments, I know we can face anything.

Speaking of Mom, she's been documenting how she's feeling throughout this pregnancy. You see, she has no idea I'm writing this book for you and her, but she's been keeping her own little notes. She recently shared some of her thoughts with me, and I had to chuckle because I feel like I'm already a few steps ahead of her, capturing every detail of this journey for you. She started writing things down on her phone back on September 30, and here's a little glimpse of what she's been experiencing.

Mom shared that she's been dealing with all-day sickness, not just morning sickness. She's also mentioned a strange metallic taste in her mouth, which is super common during pregnancy, and she's been craving certain foods. Black olives and Shake Shack burgers seem to be at the top of her list, but only the burgers from Shake Shack! She's still in love with Chick-fil-A (some things never change), and she's found comfort in frozen grapes and ginger cough drops to ease the nausea. Chipotle rice, Moby Dick rice, and plain noodles with Parmesan (no butter) are also her go-to foods lately.

Her body is working overtime to make you, and it's taking a toll. The first fourteen weeks have been rough on her, and with her uterus starting to lift and move, breathing has become a bit harder for her. But let me tell you, Mom handles it all with grace, even if she's rocking her sweatpants more often than usual. She thinks I hate it, but truthfully, as long as she's comfortable and you're healthy, I'm the happiest guy in the world.

A couple of weeks ago, during her twelfth week, Mom wrote: "Little girl, you're killing me. These last two days have been really bad, and I feel like I'm a boat in the middle of a storm. I hope it's just dehydration causing the nausea, but I am almost at my breaking point. Please settle and take whatever nutrients you need from my body and my bones and help me feel better and normal again."

Reading her words, my heart broke for all she's gone through, but it also soared at the same time—because it proved, once more, the depth of her love for you. She'd give every ounce of strength to ensure you grow healthy and strong.

That's the kind of love and sacrifice she's making for you, sweet girl. Mom knows you're strong and resilient—you've already been through so much together. From Papito's passing, wild waterslides in the Bahamas, to zip-lining adventures and 4DX movies, you've proven you're a tough little fighter.

By week fourteen, Mom said the nausea was easing up a bit, which was a relief. She still feels it every day, and she's been taking Zofran to help her manage it. She joked, "Girl, you're giving me migraines! But it's okay, because I love you." I think that's Mom's way of saying that no matter what, you're worth every challenge she's facing. She also mentioned that she got to see you kick on the ultrasound—though she couldn't feel it we all saw it, and it was such a cute, funny moment. Your little legs gave a big stretch when the sonographer was pushing down on Mom's belly to get a good look at you. Even then, you were showing us some personality!

Mom loves you so much, and even though her body is going through a lot, she's handling it all with the grace and strength of a true warrior. And just like her, I know you're going to be strong, independent, and full of love.

I catch myself daydreaming about the day you'll see these words—maybe when you're a teenager, flipping through pages out of curiosity. I hope you'll sense how deeply we believed in you, how steadfastly we fought for you, and how unwavering Mom's resolve has been from day one.

I'll never forget how Mom hit a real low point during week thirteen. While I was out flying somewhere on the West Coast, Mom's blood pressure dropped, and she felt very weak, like she could barely stand. She made an appointment to see a doctor in Damascus, and they confirmed that her blood pressure was dangerously low. The doctor told her she needed to start walking daily to improve her circulation, even though she barely has the energy to get out of bed some days. But despite how drained she was, Mom, being the warrior she is, pushed herself to walk every single day. It wasn't easy—every step felt like a battle—but she did it, for you, for me, for our family.

She also spent days trying to get in with a cardiologist. It was more precautionary than anything, but we both knew how critical it was to make sure her heart was strong enough to see this pregnancy through. Eliana, we need your mom more than anything in this world. Her health is everything to us—she's the rock of our family, the heartbeat that keeps us all together. Watching her fight through the pain and exhaustion, knowing she's doing it all for you, has made me love her even more deeply than I thought possible.

There were moments when I felt helpless. I watched her struggling, lying in bed, fighting through the nausea, and there was nothing I could do to take it away. I wanted so badly to ease her pain, but all I could do was hold her hand and remind her that she wasn't alone—that she had me, and that soon, she would have you in her arms too. And that's when it hit me: How incredible she is. She's giving everything she has to make sure you're healthy, and she never once complains. She endures it all because she knows how much you mean to both of us.

As for me, I've been flying a lot lately, mostly while Colton is with his mom. When he's with us, the house is a little crazier, but it feels so warm and full of life. It's like our family is almost complete, but not quite. We're missing one very important piece: you. Soon, when you arrive in April (or maybe March, depending on when Mom decides to have her cesarean section), we'll finally be a family of five.

I can't wait to hold you, my sweet Eliana. *I wonder what you'll look like. Will you have big brown eyes like Mom? Or maybe you'll have a head full of hair like me and your mom?* Either way, I already know one thing for sure: You're going to be my daughter, and no one will ever love you as much as I do.

Keep growing strong in Mom's belly. We love you so much, and we can't wait to meet you.

Love always,

Dad

CHAPTER TWENTY-THREE

STRENGTH IN THE STRUGGLE

October 12, 2024

Eliana, today marks a special milestone: You've turned fifteen weeks! According to the Bump app, you're growing at an incredible rate. This week, you're about the size of an apple, measuring around four inches long and weighing roughly two-and-a-half ounces. Your little body is going through some fascinating changes: Your legs are now longer than your arms, and you're busy practicing all sorts of movements, though Mom can't feel them just yet. Your skin is still translucent, but your bones are getting stronger, and the little taste buds in your mouth are beginning to form. You're getting closer and closer to being ready for the outside world, but for now, we're happy knowing you're safe and sound, growing in Mom's belly.

My dearest Eliana, today I want to share something vital with you—and with anyone reading these words—about the beautiful, unpredictable journey of life. Life has a way of surprising us, sweeping us up in waves of joy one moment and plunging us into pain the next, but it's in our response to these highs and lows that our true selves are forged. There will be times when your heart feels heavy, when the world seems to crumble beneath your feet, and doubt whispers that you can't go on. But there will also be moments of radiant, uncontainable joy—moments when happiness floods your soul, when everything aligns, and you know you're exactly where you're meant to be. How you choose to meet both—the tears and the triumphs—that's the legacy you'll leave behind. It's not the stumbles that define us, but the courage to rise again, the humility to embrace gratitude in the good times, and the strength to stand firm when you feel weakest. The world will watch, Eliana, and it will be moved by your resilience, your grace, your unwavering light. Perhaps one day you'll read this, rolling your eyes at your old man's earnest advice, but I promise you, from a heart that has weathered its own storms, that faith and perseverance can transform even the darkest nights into a brilliant dawn. Let this be your beacon, my love—and for you, dear reader, may it ignite the same hope in your own journey.

I bring this up because, I want you to know that your mom has walked through a valley of shadows these past fifteen weeks, yet she rises each day with a strength that inspires us all. She's faced profound heartbreak and loss, beginning with the passing of her dad, your Papito, a wound that cut deep, and in the same devastating week, your Nana M endured a mini-stroke, a medical scare that shook us to our core. It was a time of heavy sorrow for your mom, watching her father's health fade and her mother battle through uncertainty, their struggles unfolding almost simultaneously. And as if that weren't enough, life continued to test us with the stress of building an addition for your Nana M here at home—meant to give her comfort and space—only to be met with a contractor whose work has been sloppy and unreliable, leaving us frustrated with subpar craftsmanship and endless delays. Even you, in your growing presence, have brought challenges—heartburn, headaches, exhaustion—that weigh on her daily. Yet through it all, your mom stands resolute, a beacon of grace and courage, her spirit unbroken. She meets each curveball with a faith that turns trials into testimony, showing us that, even in our darkest moments, there is a light that refuses to dim. Let her example guide you, my love—and you, dear reader, may it remind you that strength is not the absence of struggle, but the choice to persevere.

Eliana, I hope that as you grow, you inherit so much of what makes your mom the incredible woman she is: Her patience, her determination, her beauty, both inside and out. She is truly one of the strongest people I've ever known. Even on her weakest days, she finds a way to smile, to push forward, and to keep going. I am so proud to call her my wife, and she is such an amazing stepmother to your brother, Colton. I can only imagine how incredible she will be as your mother.

Speaking of Colton, let me tell you about something that happened just today—the day you turned fifteen weeks. Colton came to me around 10:00 at night and said his stomach hurt. He showed me a lump protruding from his belly, and I immediately knew something was wrong. I called your mom downstairs to take a look, and we quickly decided to take him to the emergency room. After hours of waiting and a CT scan, we were told he had an incarcerated hernia, and we were transferred to Children's National Hospital in Washington, D.C.

It was a long and exhausting night, but Colton stood strong through it all. I watched him as they placed an IV in his left arm—only for it to go straight through the vein, causing them to switch to his right arm. I saw the fear in his eyes, the tears silently rolling down his cheeks, and my heart ached for him. He was scared, tired, and exhausted, but he never complained. Even though he didn't have the words to say it, I could see how brave he was, how he was trying to stay strong, just like I know you will someday.

It's moments like these that remind me how important it is to stay strong, even when we feel weak. Colton showed so much courage in that emergency room, and I have no doubt that you will have that same strength inside of you. Between your mom's steadfastness and your brother's bravery, I know you will grow up to be a strong, independent, and resilient young woman.

Always remember, Eliana, that in your darkest days and toughest moments, you are never alone. God is always by your side, and so are we—your mom, your brothers, and me. We will always be here, loving you, supporting you, and standing by you, no matter what life throws your way.

Keep growing, little one. We love you more than you can imagine.

Love always,

Dad

CHAPTER TWENTY-FOUR

MY SWEET LITTLE AVOCADO

October 19, 2024

My sweet little avocado, here we are at sixteen weeks, and this might just be my favorite week yet. It's not just because of your growth milestone but also because avocados have a special place in our family's heart. Your mom has always loved them, and she's been eating them more frequently this week. But it's more than that—Papito loved avocados too. When I logged into the app and saw that you're the size of an avocado today, it brought warmth and a smile to my heart, knowing that you're growing strong.

At sixteen weeks, you're about four-and-a-half inches long and weighing roughly 3.5 ounces. You're starting to develop more defined facial features, and your muscles are getting stronger—soon, Mom might even start feeling your kicks! You've got tiny toenails forming, and your heart is pumping about twenty-five quarts of blood every day. It's amazing to think about how much you've grown in just a few short weeks. You're getting ready to start making even more moves, and we can't wait to feel those little nudges from you.

Now, I have to tell you that this past Friday, Mom experienced some severe stomach pains. It worried both of us, so we decided to go to your check-up about a week early, just to make sure everything was okay. Don't worry—everything looks good with you! The doctor said that Mom might just need a little help with digestion, so they recommended mixing some MiraLAX with her Benefiber to ease some of the discomfort. It's nothing serious, but we wanted to be sure everything was fine.

They also took some blood to test for something called spina bifida. I'm not entirely sure what it is, but I certainly don't want you to have it. It's moments like these that remind me that even though we're out of the first trimester, the journey can still be scary. Any time Mom's not feeling well, or we hear stories online about someone losing their baby at sixteen or twenty weeks, it sends a chill down my spine. The very thought of losing you is too much to bear, and I pray every single day for your continued health and growth.

As we head deeper into fall, the temperature is starting to cool down. This is the fun time of year when you need a coat in the morning but can wear shorts by lunchtime. The fall colors are in full swing here in Maryland—beautiful shades of brown, red, and orange covering the trees and making the sky seem even more beautiful. It's one of my favorite times of the year, and soon Halloween will be here. I suspect you'll dress up as, well . . . a baby, naturally!

Mom has been thinking about dressing up as Winnie the Pooh, partly because she thinks it would be fun and partly because she wants to disguise her growing belly, though I don't think she looks like Winnie the Pooh at all. In fact, she's as beautiful as ever, and I can't wait to see how she looks as your belly continues to grow.

I know this chapter isn't the most exciting, sweetheart, but sometimes, that's a good thing. It's been a pretty calm and stress-free week—exactly what Mom and I want for you and for her. No drama, no worries, just a peaceful time as you continue to grow and develop into the beautiful little girl we are waiting to meet. Of course, if anything dramatic happens, I'll be sure to let you know, but for now, I'm just grateful for the calm.

And in these quiet days, I'm reminded to be thankful for every moment of peace. After all we've been through, a week of normalcy is like a sweet whisper from God, telling us He's got this under control.

I love you, kiddo. Keep growing strong.

Dad

CHAPTER TWENTY-FIVE

THROUGH THE FIRE

November 04, 2024

Hello, my beautiful Ellie,

It's been a couple of weeks since I've checked in with you, and you've been busy growing and developing into the strong little girl we're so eager to meet. Here we are at week eighteen, and it's incredible to see how much you've changed since week seventeen. You're now about the size of a bell pepper—around five-and-a-half inches long and weighing almost seven ounces. You're moving around more than ever, practicing those tiny kicks and stretches, which, soon enough, Mom might even start to feel!

Over the past couple of weeks, you've hit some big milestones in your development. During week seventeen, your skeleton was transitioning from soft cartilage to bone, a huge step in preparing for the world. Your ears were shifting into place, and you may even be able to hear sounds around you now. You might have started to recognize Mom's heartbeat and even faint noises from the outside world, like my voice when I talk to you through her belly. Your heart is now beating stronger and still pumping about twenty-five quarts of blood a day—such a powerful little engine working hard!

As you entered week eighteen, more exciting developments took place. Your sensory development is in full swing, and you're now starting to form the beginnings of fingerprints—your own unique marks in this world. The nerves in your brain are connecting with nerve endings in your body, helping you experience touch, though it's still early days for you to sense much just yet. You're growing tiny toenails and even practicing a few reflexive movements, preparing for the day you'll join us in the outside world.

I often catch myself wondering which features of Mom or me you'll inherit—her eyes and big heart, my sense of humor, or maybe a combination that will be beautifully, uniquely you.

It's been a calm few weeks, thankfully. Mom has had a chance to relax, and we've cherished this peaceful time, grateful for each quiet moment. But today, November 4, 2024, that peace came to a sudden halt.

I had just left my hotel in Los Angeles, gearing up for a busy day with three flight legs scheduled between LA and San Francisco, when I got a text from Mom that made my heart drop. All it said was, "I was just in a really bad accident." In that moment, everything else around me disappeared. A thousand thoughts and questions flooded my mind. My heart was racing, but the fact that she could text gave me a glimmer of hope.

I immediately sent her a few texts, asking if she was okay, but when she didn't respond, panic set in. I called her three or four times, and each time, there was no answer. My mind went to some dark places, imagining her on her way to the hospital, maybe even in an ambulance. Of course, my deepest fear was for you, Ellie. All I wanted was some assurance that you were both safe.

Finally, I got through to her. She answered in tears, her voice shaky and full of shock. She said she wasn't even sure how it happened—it was like she'd blacked out. The car was damaged pretty badly on the front end, and it had been a multi-vehicle accident. She was dazed, overwhelmed, and clearly rattled.

I told her to call the police, let them know she was pregnant, and get to a hospital as soon as possible. I needed to know you were okay, that she was okay. Most of our conversation was over text, and her responses were slow, which only added to my frustration and worry. I felt helpless, sitting in the back of a van with three other crew members, holding back tears, not wanting my captain to question whether I was okay to fly. But the truth was, my mind was thousands of miles away, focused solely on the two of you.

I called Nana M and asked her to go pick up Mom at the accident scene and take her to the emergency room in Germantown. Just before I took off, I learned that she was on her way to the hospital. As we flew I couldn't help but keep looking at my phone, waiting for any kind of update. I told myself not to look, that I'd prepare myself for the worst but hope for the best. I thought of Papito, praying he was watching over both of you.

Then, finally, the message came through: *"Baby's heartbeat is strong at 140 beats per minute. No bleeding or spotting. No cramping. Everything looks good."* I let out the biggest sigh of relief, probably for the first time all day. At least for that moment, I felt like I could breathe again.

Once I landed in San Francisco, I called Mom. She sounded a bit more composed, the shock beginning to wear off. I urged her to see her OB/GYN as soon as possible for follow-up, even though her current doctor at Capital Women's Care had refused to see her the day of the accident. Thankfully, she was able to get an appointment scheduled for Wednesday, November 5. She also decided it was time to look for a new OB, a decision I completely supported.

It was an emotional roller coaster of a day; one I wasn't prepared for in the slightest. Today was a reminder of just how quickly happiness can slip through our fingers, of how fragile life is. The joy and anticipation we've felt these past eighteen weeks could have been stolen from us in an instant. That's a thought I can hardly bear, and it made me realize, all over again, how deeply I love you and Mom.

Ironically, six years ago today, I posted a verse on my Facebook account:

> *"You don't know where the wind will blow, and you don't know how a baby grows inside the mother. In the same way, you don't know what God is doing or how He created everything."—Ecclesiastes 11:5.*[5]

It's a verse about mystery, faith, and trust, and today, it felt like it was written for us.

Keep fighting, my sweet girl. Mom and I will do everything we can to protect you, to cherish each moment with you, and to give you all the love we have. We're in this together, through every storm and every ray of sunshine. You've already proven you're brave, and we can't wait to hold you, to love you, and to show you how strong you truly are.

In the end, I whispered a prayer of gratitude, thanking God for safeguarding you and Mom yet again. "I Believe"—those two words came back to my mind like a gentle echo, reminding me that faith has carried us this far, and will carry us all the way.

With all my heart,

Dad

---

[5] Ecclesiastes 11:5, New International Reader's Version (NIRV).

CHAPTER TWENTY-SIX

HALF-BAKED AND FULLY LOVED

November 16, 2024

My little banana, how are you doing today? It's Saturday, November 16, 2024, and today marks a special milestone: Mom is officially halfway through her pregnancy with you. That's right, Eliana, you're half-baked! It's amazing to think that in just twenty weeks, we'll finally be holding you in our arms.

A lot has happened since my last update, so let me fill you in on everything you've been up to these past few weeks. According to the Bump, here's a detailed breakdown of how you've grown:

- Week nineteen: You were about the size of a mango, measuring six inches long and weighing around eight-and-a-half ounces. Your senses were growing sharper every day—your brain working hard to develop areas for smell, taste, hearing, vision, and touch. And your skin was starting to grow a protective coating called vernix caseosa to keep you safe and comfy in Mom's belly.

- Week twenty: And now here we are, my little banana! You're about six-and-a-half inches long and weigh around 10.2 ounces. You're busy practicing swallowing and digesting, which is helping your digestive system prepare for the world outside. Your little legs have stretched out, and you're becoming more proportional every day. It won't be long before we can feel your kicks from the outside, and trust me, we can't wait for that moment!

It hasn't been the easiest few weeks for Mom. Even at twenty weeks, she's still battling nausea, heartburn, and those just not feeling well days. But let me tell you, Ellie, your mom is incredible. She handles everything with grace and determination because she knows how special you are. Today, we're celebrating the halfway point in this journey—half of the challenges and half of the struggles, but also half of the miracles and moments of pure love.

This upcoming Wednesday, we have your anatomy scan, and I can't tell you how excited we are for it. That scan will show us every little detail—your tiny fingers and toes, the shape of your nose, and even the chambers of your heart. It's going to be one of those moments where everything feels real again, like the miracle of you growing inside Mom is too big for words.

Ellie, you are the child we prayed for, the miracle who started out as a tiny frozen embryo and has already filled our hearts with more love than we ever thought possible. Every time we think about you, we're overwhelmed by gratitude for the amazing God who gave us such a blessing.

Mom is recovering well from the nasty flu bug I unfortunately passed to her. Despite the sickness and the occasional feeling of being a "beached whale," as she puts it, Mom's spirit and beauty never wane. I see her growing every day, each change a brushstroke in the masterpiece that is your coming into being.

I cling to that phrase, "I Believe." It's like the theme song of your life, playing in the background of every joyous ultrasound and every anxious trip to the doctor, reminding us that God's promises never fail.

So, as we prepare to celebrate Christmas and welcome the New Year, I think about how blessed we are. Blessed to have each other, blessed to be your parents, and blessed to soon meet the little girl who's already brought so much love into our lives. Hold on tight, Eliana, the next chapter is just around the corner, and it's filled with the warmth of family gatherings, the laughter of your future playmates, and the love of everyone eagerly awaiting your grand entrance.

With all my love,

Dad

CHAPTER TWENTY-SEVEN

WEATHERING STORMS WITH GRACE AND GRIT

December 2 to December 8, 2024

Eliana, my little fighter,

As you reach the twenty-second week of your incredible journey, you've grown to the size of a papaya—just under a pound and around eleven inches long. You've already left your mark on our hearts, not just with the kicks and wiggles but with the resilience and hope you've sparked in our lives.

Your twenty-week anatomy scan was nothing short of breathtaking. At first, you were curled into a tight little ball, a cozy bundle of mystery. But soon, you stretched your legs dramatically over your head, making both Mom and me laugh through our awe. You were measured at exactly twelve ounces at the time—perfectly on track—and we marveled at your ten tiny fingers and toes. That moment wasn't just clinical; it was spiritual. Each scan feels like a glimpse into God's design, His careful, beautiful handiwork unfolding before our eyes.

As you've grown, so has Mom—literally. By week twenty-one, her belly measured forty-two inches around. It's been amazing to watch her body change and adapt to nurture you. Even when migraines, discomfort, and exhaustion weigh her down, she continues to press on with strength and grace. Her courage has become the heartbeat of this home.

This season has brought more than just physical growth; it's tested our emotional and spiritual limits too. Our home construction project, meant to build a live-in addition for your Nana M, spiraled into a sixteen-month saga filled with frustration and loss. We invested more than $200,000, only to have our contractor vanish, taking $121,700 of our money with him. The betrayal was deep, but our faith never faltered.

Then came Thanksgiving. We gathered under a rainy Maryland sky, surrounded by family and friends, grateful not for perfection but for promise. That day, we shared laughter over a cinnamon sugar pizza pie—our little Friendsgiving tradition. It was a moment to breathe, to enjoy simple joys in the midst of ongoing trials.

But just days later, on Sunday, December 1, a pipe burst in the construction zone. We had just returned from Christmas shopping when Mom noticed low water pressure. The next thing I knew, I was racing into the crawl space in freezing weather, battling to stop the flooding. Water surged through the unfinished addition, soaking insulation and pooling along the subfloor. Armed with a shop vac and sheer determination, I worked for hours, every muscle aching, as the cold bit at my fingers. The damage felt like a cruel punctuation mark on an already difficult chapter.

Around the same time, we learned that Mom's car—a Highlander that held years of memories—was declared a total loss after her recent accident. That vehicle had been more than just transportation; it was a vessel of our story. Losing it was like saying goodbye to a chapter we hadn't finished writing.

Still, we pressed on. "For we walk by faith, not by sight."[6] That verse has become our mantra. Through tears, setbacks, and sleepless nights,

---

[6] 2 Corinthians 5:7, English Standard Version Revision 2016 (ESV).

we've kept our eyes on the promise of your arrival. Every challenge is reshaping us, preparing us not just to welcome you, but to create a life of resilience, love, and unshakable trust in God's timing.

By weeks twenty-two and twenty-three, you were developing rapidly—covered in soft lanugo, your senses awakening, and your ears beginning to recognize our voices. I hope the sound of my voice brings you comfort, a sense of connection to the world that's waiting to meet you.

You, Eliana, are our little warrior, a living symbol of hope forged through adversity. We weather these storms not for what we can regain but for the beautiful life we're building with you. When you finally arrive, you'll find a home built on more than just wood and nails—it's built on faith, grit, and a love that refuses to break.

With all my love, forever and always,

Dad

CHAPTER TWENTY-EIGHT

FEELING THE KICK

December 14, 2024

Eliana, you're twenty-four weeks along, and today, I felt you kick for the first time. Lying beside Mom, feeling that little flutter was like whispering directly to my heart, an instant connection that I cannot fully describe. It was the first true interaction between us, even if just a swift nudge separated by skin and warmth, but it felt like a profound conversation in the language of love and little kicks.

I closed my eyes for a moment, letting that tiny jolt sink in. *This*, I thought, *is what we've prayed for.* It was both gentle and mighty, reminding me of how powerful new life can be.

December 21, 2024

Now, as of December 21, 2024, you've hit twenty-five weeks, blossoming beautifully to the size of a cauliflower. You measure about thirteen-and-a-half inches long and weigh around a pound and a half. Your body is busy developing; you're gaining more fat to keep you cozy and your senses are sharpening each day. The sound of our voices, the gentle hum of daily life—it's all becoming part of your little world.

This week also marks another significant milestone—not just for you but for our family's future adventures. Mom and I faced a whirlwind of decisions as we finalized the purchase of a 2019 Infiniti QX60. It wasn't smooth sailing, but issues with the dealership and even a last-minute dead battery couldn't deter us. This car isn't just a vehicle; it's a promise of homecomings, of drives to Michigan, and of the countless journeys we'll share. It's the car that will bring you home and be part of your earliest memories.

Christmas is just around the corner, and the air is filled with a mix of excitement and the crisp promise of new beginnings. We're nearly done with our holiday preparations, a time made even sweeter by the anticipation of your arrival. This season is about joy and gratitude, and even amidst challenges—like the stressful car buying or the ongoing construction woes—we find reasons to smile and be thankful.

It feels like every day leading up to Christmas is another chance to celebrate not just the birth of Jesus but also the miracle growing inside Mom, like all of these traditions are a rehearsal for the joy we'll share next year when we're blessed to hold you in our arms.

Hold on tight, Ellie; the next chapter is just around the corner, filled with the warmth of family gatherings, the laughter of your future playmates, and the love of everyone eagerly awaiting your grand entrance.

With love,

Dad

CHAPTER TWENTY-NINE

A PROMISE OF JOYFUL CHRISTMASES TO COME

December 24, 2024

December 24, 2024, brought with it more than the festive cheer of Christmas Eve; it marked a milestone in our family's journey. Mom finally announced to the world through a heartfelt social media post that she's six months pregnant with you, our little princess, Eliana. The thought that in just one year you'll be here with us, experiencing your first Christmas, fills me with indescribable joy.

There's something magical about sharing the news with everyone—almost like we're inviting the entire world to believe with us, to hope with us, and to celebrate you with us.

This time next year, you'll be nine months old, the day before your very first Christmas. We plan to take you ice-skating; yes, even though you might just be learning to walk, I believe you'll do wonderfully—perhaps even better than me! I've already started buying gifts for you. They're wrapped and waiting, a promise of the magical moments we'll share when you're finally here.

Christmas is going to be spectacular next year, a family of five together for the first time. It will be the best Christmas gift Mom has ever given me. She's already given me an ornament with a promise: Next Christmas, you'll be cuddling with me all day. I'm holding onto that ornament as a reminder of the promise made, a token of the future joys we'll share.

I can't explain how comforting it is to see a baby ornament hanging on our tree, a physical symbol that yes, you are coming, and yes, we have so much love waiting.

December 25, 2024

Merry Christmas, My Little Princess

Let me be the first to wish you Merry Christmas! Christ has been born, and Santa Claus has made his magical journey. By this time next year, you'll be trying to unwrap presents; I'll make sure not to use too much tape, so it's easy for you.

Our family tradition involves a lavish breakfast, though this year, it will be bittersweet as Colton will head back to his mom's house at 11 a.m. I'm sure that by this time next year, you'll be snuggled up and possibly napping after a morning filled with excitement, draped in a brand-new plush Louis Vuitton blanket—a surprise your mom doesn't know about yet.

Merry Christmas, my sweet princess. I love you so immensely. I feel incredibly blessed to have you as my daughter and to have such a beautiful family. Whenever you doubt the goodness in life, remember this chapter. During my darkest days, when I struggled to find a reason to continue, God provided a miracle in you and a second chance at a family—a chance to love and cherish a family in ways I've never known before.

When you arrive, you'll experience an overwhelming amount of love from your mom, your brothers, and me. I have no doubt that when you become a mom yourself, you'll instill the same feeling of love in your children.

Merry Christmas today and every day, my sweet little princess. Your arrival will complete our family, and we can't wait to meet you.

As I set the last gift beneath the tree, I whispered a silent prayer of thanks, letting my heart swell with the knowledge that this time of waiting is weaving hope, faith, and love into every breath we take.

Love,

Daddio

CHAPTER THIRTY

CELEBRATING MILESTONES AMIDST UNEXPECTED TWISTS

December 28, 2024

Hello, my little kale! Today marks week twenty-six of our journey together, and with each day, your presence becomes more pronounced. You're nearly fourteen inches long now and weigh about one-and-two-thirds pounds. Your movements are stronger and more defined—Mom can feel you stretching and kicking, maybe even getting the hiccups, which tickle more than you know!

Your development is truly astounding. Your lungs are preparing for those first breaths of air, and your ears are fine-tuning, enhancing your ability to hear. By now, you might recognize my voice and respond with little jabs of excitement or curiosity.

Meanwhile, Mom is experiencing the physical reminders that you are growing. Her belly expands each week, stretching her skin and causing some discomfort. But despite the occasional aches, she glows with the beauty of impending motherhood, radiating a mix of resilience and grace.

Our post-Christmas journey to Michigan brought both joy and challenges. We were all set for a baby shower, organized lovingly by Nana W and Aunt Sarah, but life had a few curveballs in store for us. First, there were the cake pops—those adorable little treats Mom had ordered specially from a bakery in Las Vegas. They were supposed to be shaped like babies, complete with little bottles and hats, a perfect touch for the celebration. However, the bakery called us at the last minute, on the Friday before the shower, to cancel our order because they couldn't fulfill it in time. This was a disappointment, especially since these unique cake pops were something Mom had been excited about.

Then there was the saga with the cake from Meijer. We had ordered a marble cake to please everyone's taste at the shower, but we received a call from the store saying they couldn't provide the cake we wanted due to a stock issue. I was initially frustrated—so much so that I called Meijer to express my disappointment. Fortunately, they were accommodating and agreed to bake a different flavor. It wasn't what we planned, but it reminded us that flexibility is key.

The day of the shower, more unexpected news came our way. Papa and Grammy Barb were down with a head cold, and Sarah, integral to the planning, couldn't attend because her baby was sick. Despite these setbacks, the celebration was filled with love and laughter. Aunt Jenny, her kids, Papa, Grammy Barb, Aunt Nicki, her kids, and Josh were all there. You received so many thoughtful gifts, each one a testament to how loved you already are.

It wasn't exactly the Pinterest-perfect event we'd envisioned, but in a way, it was better—real, raw, and overflowing with the warmth of family who stood by us through every high and low.

This rollercoaster of events didn't just teach us about the unpredictability of life—it showcased the strength and adaptability of your family. We handle what comes our way, finding joy and gratitude even in less-than-ideal circumstances.

As we look forward to your arrival, remember this: Life doesn't always follow the planned route. But with faith and the support of loved ones, every challenge becomes a shared adventure, every setback a story of resilience.

So here's to growing, adapting, and preparing—for your arrival and all the beautiful chaos that comes with it. We can't wait to meet you, to see your smile, to hear your laugh, and to introduce you to the world that awaits.

Love always,

Dad

CHAPTER THIRTY-ONE

PERSEVERING THROUGH THE PANDEMIC'S ECHOES

January 06, 2025

Hello, my little rutabaga! This week marks your twenty-seventh week inside Mom's growing belly. You're about 14.4 inches long now and weigh nearly two pounds. Your little body is getting stronger every day; your brain is developing rapidly, your eyes are beginning to open, and you might even start to dream!

As we start this new year, we find ourselves navigating a rough patch. It reminds me a bit of how things began right after Mom and I started dating, back when I went to Singapore for my Boeing 777 type rating and training. During that time, a little virus known as COVID-19 began to emerge in Central Asia. It wasn't long before the virus spread worldwide, eventually reaching the United States and creating unprecedented challenges globally.

COVID-19, a novel coronavirus, quickly escalated into a pandemic, profoundly impacting every aspect of daily life. Countries shut down, travel came to a standstill, economies faltered, and health systems were overwhelmed. Social distancing and masks became part of everyday routines, as did uncertainty and fear. The world had to adapt rapidly, learning to cope with the immense pressures of a global health crisis that affected millions.

Fast-forward to January 2025, and the echoes of that pandemic are still felt in our home. Mom, unfortunately, has been diagnosed with COVID-19. Since she's pregnant, she can't take the usual medications to alleviate her symptoms, which makes this time particularly tough. Dave battling the Type-A flu adds to the challenge. Our house feels like a zone of perpetual recovery, with tissues, coughs, and concern filling the air.

Sometimes, when I hear those coughs in the night, my heart clenches, and I whisper a prayer: "God, keep them safe—keep Eliana safe." Faith has carried us through so much already, and I trust it'll carry us through this too.

But amidst this chaos, I am reminded of the resilience and strength both you and Mom possess. Mom, your warrior spirit is undeniable. Through every sneeze and every tough night, she shows incredible fortitude, all while nurturing you, making sure you're growing healthy and strong. Your journey together through these times is a testament to the enduring spirit of our family.

Here are some heartfelt words from Mom herself, reflecting on this challenging yet miraculous time:

"Yesterday you turned twenty-seven weeks . . . Time has flown by, and I know the next twelve to thirteen weeks will pass even quicker. Thankfully, you've eased up on giving me nausea, headaches, and heartburn. But now, as you grow bigger, every cough, sneeze, or laugh seems to make me pee a little—a small price to pay to feel you moving. Wearing this Zio heart monitor to ensure my heart stays strong for you has been tough, almost as tough as the nausea. It's getting hard to breathe sometimes, like I'm suffocating. Yet feeling you move and kick, especially at night and in the early mornings, reassures me you're safe and happy, even though it keeps me awake. And now, I've caught

COVID too, putting us both through the wringer. But I know nothing can keep you down; you're going to be a tough little warrior princess. We keep wondering who you'll take after more—will you have my hair color, or your dad's eyes, or maybe a mix of both our personalities? No matter what, you'll be beautiful and uniquely special."

This period isn't just about overcoming illness; it's a reminder of how we, as a family and a global community, face and adapt to challenges. COVID-19 changed the world, but it also showed us how capable we are of resilience and transformation.

So here's to you, Ellie, growing bravely in a world that's full of surprises. Here's to Mom, who battles through every hardship with a smile for you. And here's to the new year, filled with hope and the promise of health and happiness.

Keep growing strong, my sweet girl. We are all in this together, and we can't wait to meet you.

Love always,

Dad

CHAPTER THIRTY-TWO

RUNNING ON FAITH, NOT ON EMERGENCY HEAT

January 08, 2025

Hello, my resilient little one! As we embark on week twenty-eight of our journey together, you are growing impressively. You now measure almost the size of an eggplant, about 14.7 inches long and weighing around 2.2 pounds. Inside Mom's belly, you're refining your brain connections, blinking, dreaming, and even regulating your own body temperature.

This week, Mom's body has been adapting to your growth. Her uterus has expanded well above her belly button, causing discomfort but also marvel at the life blossoming within her. Yet, it's your vigorous kicks and lively jabs, often sharp enough to make her gasp, that light up her world and bring immense joy amidst our ongoing challenges.

Feeling those kicks is like receiving postcards from you, letting us know you're thriving despite the storms we face on the outside.

Speaking of challenges, they seem to follow us relentlessly. Just when we thought we might catch a breath, our home's heat pump decided to give up in the heart of winter, forcing our air handler into emergency heat mode to combat the biting cold. The temperatures have been swinging wildly, from a chilling low of fourteen degrees to a more bearable forty-four degrees on some days. Replacing the heat pump/Air conditioning system was an unexpected financial hit, drawing heavily from our emergency fund—a vital lesson in preparedness we hope to pass on to you.

Amid these mechanical upheavals, your development remains wonderfully on track. You're developing a sense of balance—knowing which way is up and down as you prepare to eventually navigate the world outside.

This week also brought the end of Mom's heart monitoring saga. After weeks of documenting every flutter and rush, her monitor has finally come off. The relief on Mom's face was obvious, yet the wait for the cardiologist's report adds a suspenseful layer to our ongoing journey.

The glucose test marked another significant milestone this week. Mom tackled the challenge of downing a super sugary drink to ensure her body is processing sugar effectively—a crucial step for both of your health. Thankfully, the results were normal, but not without the comic grimace of determination on Mom's face as she braved through the taste.

We also discovered that Mom is slightly anemic, a common but manageable twist in pregnancy, indicating she needs more iron. It's a minor hiccup in the grand tapestry of this journey, easily addressed with a good diet and supplements.

Our faith remains our strongest ally amid these trials. Despite the household breakdowns and health scares, we are reminded daily that with faith, resilience, and the support of loved ones, we can navigate any storm.

I remind myself every day: "I Believe." That small but mighty statement has become our anchor, holding us firm whenever chaos threatens to toss us around.

This chapter of our lives, filled with unexpected turns and educational moments, reinforces the incredible strength and resilience being nurtured within you. Every kick and heartbeat fortifies our resolve to meet life's uncertainties with grace and courage.

As we close this week, we're filled with gratitude for your health and the joy you bring into our lives, even from the quiet of the womb. We look forward to each new day with you, each challenge, and each blessing. Keep growing strong, my little warrior. The excitement to meet you grows with each passing day.

With all the love in the world,

Dad

CHAPTER THIRTY-THREE

STRENGTH IN THE WAITING

January 21 to 30, 2025

My precious Eliana,

We've made it to week twenty-nine, and you're growing faster than I ever imagined. At this stage, you're right around the size of a butternut squash—about fifteen inches long and weighing nearly two and a half pounds. Each day, your movements become more pronounced, your tiny jabs and squirms a constant reminder of how real and close you are. It's astonishing to think your brother Colton arrived at twenty-nine weeks and two days, and here you are, surpassing that milestone, with only seventy days remaining until we meet, if all goes according to plan for your March 31 C-section.

This week, your development is nothing short of miraculous. You're further refining your senses and practicing your breathing. Soon, you'll open those eyes more often, peering into the world that awaits outside Mom's belly. The Bump app confirms you're steadily gaining weight, preparing those little lungs for that first precious cry.

Meanwhile, life beyond Mom's womb presses on with challenges that test our faith and resilience. When the electric bill arrived—$1,375 for one month after our furnace gave out—I went to the shower and broke down. After all we've endured these past few months, I'd met my match and finally felt the weight of it all crush me. I found myself asking, *How does Mom stay so strong?* I felt helpless, alone, defeated. Was God testing my faith again? I've weathered darker storms than this, yet in that moment I had to admit to Him that my boat might sink under the swell of bills and breakdowns.

But then I remembered the words of our song, "I Believe."[7] I whispered them through tears, clinging to every promise those lyrics carry. I took a deep breath, collected myself, and prayed: "Lord, this storm will not break me. You hold my oars." In that quiet surrender, strength returned. I knew we would endure this trial—and emerge on the other side more steadfast and united than before. Through humility and faith, we trust that God's provision will arrive just when we need it. We don't have to fix everything on our own; He guides us through the waves, and I believe He will guide us safely to shore.

All the while, Mom presses forward, though I can see the cracks forming in her bravado. She's washing and folding your clothes, removing the tags, assembling your stroller and bassinet. Her excitement shows through the fatigue—she's finally meeting her baby girl soon. And no matter how many setbacks we face, the thought of your arrival brightens our spirit, again and again.

The week ended with both setbacks and solutions. We replaced the furnace and air conditioning units entirely, ensuring you'll have a cozy home to grow in for the next fifteen to twenty years. However, my car's uncertain future lingers, pushing us to weigh whether we patch it up or let it go. As we do with everything, we lean on faith. God doesn't bring us this far to abandon us, and we trust in His timing.

I've also been contemplating a significant career move—accepting an upgrade to captain. It promises better pay and fewer flights, but at the cost of relinquishing my hard-earned seniority and flexible schedule.

---

7   Phil Wickham, "I Believe."

It's an ongoing mental tug-of-war: *Do I work harder now to maintain our stability, or do I grab this promotion and trust that sacrificing schedule control is worth the financial relief?* Faith remains our anchor, guiding us through each decision.

January 30, 2025

Stepping into week thirty means you're changing at lightning speed. According to the Bump, you'll be thickening up, practicing your breathing more diligently, and you might even start responding more eagerly to Mom's voice—our voices. We can't help but get excited about Thursday, January 31: The day of our three-dimensional 8K ultrasound session that will generate an AI-enhanced image of your precious little face. My heart flutters at the mere thought, tears welling as I imagine the overwhelming emotion Mom and I will feel when we finally see you in such vivid detail.

But as always, life tosses us curveballs. On Tuesday, January 28, Mom heard back from her cardiologist. We've been frustrated with their poor communication—an understatement—and their verdict is that Mom has tachycardia, though they can't specify the type. They recommend she start on a beta-blocker named Metoprolol, pending approval from her OB. The doctor didn't even mention the dosage, leaving us uncomfortably in the dark. We decided to wait until Mom's next OB appointment, trusting her OB's judgment. It's hard not to be unsettled when someone's so cavalier about medication that affects both Mom and you, but we're learning to navigate the unknown.

Then came Thursday, January 30—a day we'd long anticipated. It began with Mom's routine OB checkup (they're now every two weeks). In a rush of relief, her OB wholeheartedly endorsed Metoprolol and promptly contacted the cardiologist's office to nail down the dosage before sending the prescription to the pharmacy. After weeks of runaround, progress felt liberating. Mom and I treated ourselves to breakfast at The Original Pancake House, one of the oldest restaurants on Rockville Pike, where we tried to block out our worries. I devoured a soft, sweet cinnamon roll and a jalapeño omelet alongside a stack of pancakes; Mom, never to be outdone, had six pancakes. It was far too much food, but we treasured the rare pleasure of simply chatting, unburdened by stress for an hour and a half.

Soon, though, came the main event—our trip to Little Bellies for your three-dimensional ultrasound. We arrived around 12:15 p.m., took a seat for about five minutes, and then found ourselves in the back room where Mom lay down. The ultrasound tech slathered her belly in warm gel, and the excitement soared. We felt on the brink of tears, knowing we were just moments from glimpsing you.

But you, my dear, had your own agenda. Despite being head down, your head on Mom's right side and feet near her left hip, you stretched your neck back to look straight up whenever the wand got near you. A twenty-five-minute session ballooned into an hour of trying everything—rolling Mom from side to side, making her laugh, having her drink water, prodding your position. You held your ground—perhaps a little early sign of your independent spirit. Eventually, the tech triumphed, and we captured a short forty-five second video. You lifted your tiny hand, waved your fingers as if to greet us, and then yawned—an endearing gesture that instantly misted my eyes. Mom laughed and smiled, and in that second, I felt an avalanche of love flood my heart. It was the clearest, most mesmerizing look at your face—delicate lips, soft features, and the sweetest yawn I've ever witnessed.

I love you my sweet French Fry,

Dad

CHAPTER THIRTY-FOUR

WAVES AND WONDERS

February 1 to 16, 2025

Now we await the 8K AI version of that image. I'm a bit giddy, mainly because I'm going to get it first and plan on having it professionally printed on a twenty-six by twenty-six-inch piece of metal. I'll keep the secret until February 16, your Mom's Maryland baby shower with her closest friends, where I'll place the picture on an easel. I can't wait for the moment she walks in, sees your beautifully rendered features, and realizes who she's staring at. That single memory will be worth every challenge we've faced.

Later that day, I picked up Mom's prescription, and we excitedly shared your ultrasound photos with your brothers. Colton lit up, calling you pretty, while Dave, a tad unsure, simply said, "Oh, that's nice." We laugh, realizing a three-dimensional color ultrasound is quite a leap from the black-and-white images he's used to. But beneath his reserved response, he loves you deeply.

February 16, 2025

On February 5, at 12:22 p.m., the AI-generated image arrived. The moment I saw your newly enhanced face, I fell for you all over again. Your sleeping eyes, your soft cheeks—technology might only approximate your real appearance, but I have no doubt you'll surpass this digital glimpse in beauty. Keeping this surprise from Mom has been excruciating, but I'm resolved not to spoil that magical reveal at the shower.

Then came February 10, a day of unexpected fear. I was away in Saint Martin for work when a text popped up on my phone at 7:15 p.m.: "Don't freak out, I'm going to the hospital." Mom's oxygen had dropped to 92 percent, and Dr. Spector urged her to head straight to the ER to rule out a pulmonary embolism. My heart pounded, stranded so far from home. She endured nearly five hours in a congested waiting room, courtesy of a cyberattack that diverted Frederick's emergency room patients to Holy Cross and Shady Grove. She was finally monitored, revealing you were okay, and eventually, near midnight, she chose to go home, exhausted but somewhat reassured.

On February 13, a mere three days later, Mom visited Capital Women's Care again, and the practice owner decided she needed another immediate scan at Shady Grove Hospital. True to her nature, Mom insisted on grabbing lunch at Moby Dick first—her little anchor of normalcy amid the hospital shuffle. They took her to the triage bay, leaving me outside, powerless yet again. While waiting, Mom jotted down notes to you, dear Eliana:

> Aw Eliana, you are thirty-two weeks and two days today, when Mommy had to go to the hospital. I felt like I couldn't breathe and it was a crazy night. They wanted to make sure I didn't have a pulmonary embolism, so they took blood and then put monitors on my tummy to make sure you were okay. You, being stubborn, kept moving but finally we got a good read on you and you were all healthy.
>
> When we went for your 4D sonogram (1/30) you did not want to cooperate. Your face was right up against the placenta and we couldn't see your beautiful little face. Finally, after twenty minutes, we were able to get you to move and we saw your sweet yawn and waves with your little fingers; it made daddy tear up. Your little lips and chin are so precious; we can't wait to meet you.
>
> Eliana, this hasn't been easy for me, from the very beginning. I woke up today feeling like I can't breathe, and this is normal. My oxygen levels drop, my heart rate goes up sometimes, it's so uncomfortable. Looking back, I don't know how we did it. Shots every day, surgery, more shots, weeks of extreme sickness, heart

issues, breathing issues, but I know all of it will be forgotten the day you are here and we see your beautiful little face. I love feeling your kicks (the soft ones, not the jabbing Ultimate Fighting Championship [UFC] ones, lol) and sometimes I can feel your heart beating down there."

Eventually, they decided to perform a CT scan to rule out a pulmonary embolism. The debate arose over covering Mom's belly with a lead blanket—designed to shield sensitive areas from X-ray radiation—because reflections from the lead can sometimes deflect rays unpredictably. In the end, they chose a compromise, covering half her belly; it was the most agonizing few minutes, deciding how best to protect you. Thankfully, the CT took only two minutes, and after a nerve-wracking hour-long wait, the results were unremarkable—a precious word that meant you and Mom were safe.

Two days later, on the day you turned thirty-three weeks, we were back at Shady Grove—this time for a planned and much happier occasion: Touring the labor and delivery floor. We viewed the Mommy & Me room, your temporary hotel suite, so to speak—a cozy space where your new world will begin, visited by friends and loved ones. It was surreal, envisioning you in those corridors, wrapped snugly in your first swaddle.

The following day, February 16, was a baby shower hosted by Mom's Damascus friends, Ty and Leslie. They had transformed Leslie's home with meticulous care—stunning balloon arches, heartwarming decorations, and an inviting array of sandwiches, soups, and cupcakes from Panera Bread. But as Mom and I pulled into the driveway, my heart wasn't focused on the food or the décor.

We were one of the first to arrive, and I could feel my pulse quicken. This was the moment. The moment Mom would lay eyes on the 8K image of Eliana for the very first time.

I wasn't sure how she would react—how could I be? I'd been holding onto that photo for days, keeping it close, waiting for the right time to reveal it. Now that moment had arrived. As we approached the front door, the anticipation was eating me alive. Through the glass, I could already see it—your image, Eliana, glowing in the center of the room like a beacon. I silently prayed that Mom wouldn't spot it too soon. I wanted her to step into the room and *feel* the moment—not rush past it.

As she crossed the threshold, she paused. Her eyes moved slowly, taking in every detail. The hours Ty and Leslie had poured into making the space magical had paid off. It was breathtaking. But it was more than that—it was sacred. And then her gaze fell upon *you*.

Right in the heart of it all, framed perfectly among the decorations, was the lifelike image of your face. The room stilled, as if time itself held its breath. Mom turned back to me with wide, trembling eyes and whispered, *"Is that her?"*

It wasn't quite the reaction I had imagined. But in that moment, it was perfectly her. No dramatic outburst. No flood of tears. Just quiet awe, as her heart caught up with what her eyes were seeing. She was trying to process it all—the beauty, the meaning, the fact that I had been holding onto this image, waiting to surprise her. I don't think it hit her fully until a few moments later.

Throughout the party, I caught her glancing back at that photo—again and again. There was something unspoken in her expression every time. Wonder. Love. Maybe even a touch of disbelief. What was she thinking as she stared into the face of the little girl who was still growing inside her?

For nearly four hours, Mom celebrated you, beaming beneath the effusive love of everyone who came. Though completely exhausted by the time we loaded the gifts into our car, she radiated pure, contented joy.

And as we drove away that night, her hand resting quietly on her belly, I knew: something had shifted. You weren't just a hope or a heartbeat anymore. You were *real*. And the journey was just beginning.

Meanwhile, each passing week showcases your remarkable growth. At another ultrasound, the doctor found you head down, facing Mom's spine, weighing in at a healthy five pounds—a testament to how well you're growing despite the daily discomforts Mom endures. We finally pinned down your official C-section appointment: March 31 at 12:30 p.m. That knowledge brings relief, though it also stirs anxiety over the unpredictability of surgery. The thought of losing either you or Mom haunts me, but I cling to hope and faith.

Only thirty-five days remain now, and I'm wrapping up one of my final February work trips. I plan to spend March by Mom's side, double-checking every detail, ensuring your nursery is perfect. Reflecting on everything we've endured—from financial strains to emergency hospital visits—my heart brims with gratitude and anticipation. The moment we see you, all stress, all worry will vanish under the weight of sheer love for you, our beautiful, beloved daughter.

I love you, Eliana, more than words can express. Thank you for being our light in the darkness, the reason we persevere through every challenge, holding onto faith that guides us through every twist of this journey.

With unwavering love,

Dad

CHAPTER THIRTY-FIVE

EMBRACING THE FINAL STRETCH WITH FAITH

March 1, 2025

My sweet Eliana,

We've reached week thirty-five of this incredible journey, and you're now about the size of a pineapple—close to eighteen inches long and weighing in around five and a half pounds, give or take. It's hard to believe how quickly time has passed. Just five weeks (maybe even less) until we meet you face-to-face.

This week also coincides with Mom's thirty-seventh birthday, which we celebrated in our own little way—an odd mix of ordinary errands and tender gratitude. We spent a lazy morning wandering through IKEA, on the hunt for a pair of chairs to place in the upstairs room where, soon enough, we'll cuddle you in the quiet hours of the night. Mom envisions a calm corner with a soft chair, a place to hold you close while gazing out the window at the moonlit sky. We found two that we liked, and though we didn't bring them home immediately, I returned later that week to pick them up—yet another step in preparing the house to welcome you with warmth and comfort.

But in typical fashion, a simple quest for chairs was just the beginning. We followed our IKEA trip with a stop at Costco, an adventure in itself. I hope, for your sake, we don't bring you there too often—especially on weekends—because the crowds can feel like a carnival of chaos. My patience sometimes flies out the window in those aisles, but we managed to grab what we needed. Afterward, I treated Mom and your brothers, Colton and Dave, to lunch at Copper Canyon Grill in Germantown's Rio shopping area. It was one of those small celebrations for Mom's birthday—just us, some good food, and a moment to sit down together.

Mom ordered a cheeseburger that arrived a little undercooked—a rare moment where she actually sent something back. Dave went for his usual chicken dish, Colton tried some linguine, and I, despite my earlier plan to order something light, ended up with chicken and waffles—and oh, were they worth every syrupy bite. When we got home later that evening, Colton excitedly opened a new gift he had bought for himself, and I took him to church while Mom rested. She spent much of the night sorting through your clothes again, always keen to make sure every little sock and outfit is in the perfect place. The day closed with a slice of Bundt cake Nana W had bought for Mom's birthday. Nana W and Mom share a special cake buddy relationship—both always ready to indulge in sweet treats to celebrate life's moments. Over the weekend, Papa also sent Mom a box of chocolate-covered fruit, another small token of how loved she is.

Just a few days later, on Wednesday, Mom had a doctor's appointment and a sonogram at Capital Women's Care. In that familiar exam room, we heard your heart gallop along at 136 beats per minute—music to our ears, though they decided not to measure your weight this time. Mom received an RSV shot to protect you from respiratory infections once you arrive, and later that evening, I went to our local clinic for a TDAP injection to stave off whooping cough. You'll come into this world without any immunity, so we're both doing whatever we can to keep you safe.

Week thirty-six crept up swiftly, bringing the usual routine of Mom and me glancing at the Bump app on Saturday morning to check your growth. By then, Mom was truly feeling the weight of these last few weeks—her hips beginning to ache, her breathing growing more labored. She believes you might already be dropping, tucking yourself lower, pressing and stretching her pelvis. While normal, the anticipation of how painful it might be once real labor sets in weighs on her mind.

Even so, we found the energy to do more around the house, decorating corners that have been untouched for nearly three years since we moved in. It's odd timing, but it feels right—like we're making a final, loving nest for you.

Still, the hardships Mom faces with her heart and breathing persist. At our appointment on March 13, they finally measured you via ultrasound, declaring you a solid seven pounds. That revelation explained the new tightness in Mom's belly—no wonder she's feeling short of room! The ultrasound tech spent a good thirty minutes trying to capture your practice breaths, which at this stage show how your lungs are rehearsing for the real deal. Mom struggled during the sonogram, wrestling with nausea and the aches of lying still. The tech also mentioned that you have noticeable hair on your head already—a detail that made Mom's eyes shine. She endured it all for a glimpse of you, and the love in her eyes when they said you were perfectly healthy was priceless.

What also emerged during these doctor visits is a comedic (and somewhat endearing) nickname I've given you: French Fry. Don't ask me where it came from. Perhaps I just have a habit of summoning random food nicknames—Colton is often Cookie, and Dave is simply Dave, I guess. At seven pounds, a French fry might be a funny misnomer, but it makes Mom chuckle, and it fills me with silly joy to have this personal label for you while you're nestled in the womb.

We have only a few short weeks left. Nana W arrives from Michigan soon, just after Mom's thirty-seven-week appointment, and we're racing to finalize everything—car seat installation, selecting a pediatrician, and tidying the house for the biggest event of our lives. The tension of the final countdown mingles with a sense of wonder, like the calm before a storm we've long prayed for.

What underpins every busy day and worry-filled night is our unwavering faith in God. After all the heartbreak—losing Papito, the fiasco with our contractor, the death of our HVAC System, Mom's car accident, and repeated hospital visits—Mom remains steadfast in her belief that each challenge is part of a greater plan. She walks, at times blindly, through these storms, but always anchored to the knowledge that the Holy Spirit keeps her afloat. I truly believe Papito, from heaven, handpicked you for us to continue his legacy, to fill the space of sorrow with a renewed light only you can bring.

So, here we stand at week thirty-six, fully aware that life can still throw punches, but finding solace in the knowledge that you, sweet Eliana, are thriving. As Mom trudges through these final days of aches and breathlessness, her spirit glows bright with anticipation for your arrival. The doctor says you're head-down and in perfect position, your weight is healthy, and that's all we could ask for. The storms we have weathered will only make your first cry that much sweeter. And with each small stroke of preparation—folding your onesies, hanging up pictures, whispering your little nickname—our hearts fill with hope, eager for the instant we can hold you against our chests and welcome you into a family that loves you more than words could ever convey.

We're nearly there, my darling. Just a few more steps in this grand adventure, a final handful of days until the day we finally see your eyes and kiss your tiny forehead. And in that moment, every trial, every heartache, will melt away, replaced by the purest love I've known.

With all my love and unbreakable faith,

Dad

CHAPTER THIRTY-SIX

HOLDING OUR BREATH, TRUSTING OUR FAITH

March 22, 2025

My precious Eliana,

We've made it to week thirty-seven, and you're growing faster than I ever imagined. At this stage, you're right around the size of a watermelon melon—about eighteen inches long and weighing nearly seven-and-a-half pounds. Each day, your movements become more pronounced, your tiny jabs and squirms a constant reminder of how real and close you are. It's astonishing to think that your arrival could happen at any moment, and we're caught in a whirlwind of preparations, emotions, and prayers.

The week began with our usual Saturday focus: Finalizing the house for your grand entrance. Mom can't slow down, driven by an almost frenetic energy to tidy, organize, and repurpose spaces. She's determined to make every nook just right for her soon-to-arrive baby girl. But tensions flared that morning—there was some friction between Mom, Nana M, and me over how to rearrange Nana M's belongings in the basement. Emotions ran high, prompting Mom and me to gather your brothers, Colton and Dave, and step out for a breather.

We spent the next few hours at World Market returning some items before hitting a few more stores in search of a small entryway table. It's strange how a modest piece of furniture can reset the tone of an entire day, but that's exactly what happened when we found the perfect table and faux flower arrangement at Target. Mom's relief and excitement were unmistakable, and we headed home with renewed spirits. We assembled the table in the foyer, instantly transforming the mood—small touches that remind us a loving, happy home is built in the little details.

Of course, Mom couldn't stop there. True to form, she marched straight to the basement, determined to move Nana M's things to the garage so your brothers could have a designated play area. Her zeal still amazes me—even this close to delivering you. By the time Sunday came, we tried to relax, but Monday brought the usual routine . . . or so it seemed.

Monday, March 17—St. Patrick's Day—unfolded differently than expected. The morning was deceptively normal: I dropped Colton off at school while Mom got Dave ready for the bus, then I swung by IKEA for a quick return. But around noon, as I sat at the kitchen counter, fine-tuning this manuscript, a chilling secret surfaced. Mom, with a voice barely above a whisper, confessed she'd called her OB/GYN. What she hadn't told me—what she'd buried beneath layers of denial—was that she hadn't felt you move for two whole days. You, our vibrant little acrobat, our constant reminder of life, had gone silent.

My world tilted. A cold dread gripped my chest, squeezing until I could barely breathe. How could this happen? Your kicks, your rolls—they were the heartbeat of our hope. Now, nothing. Jokes about grabbing hospital bags or quips about "Here we go again" died on our lips, replaced by a suffocating fear. Mom tried drinking orange juice, hoping to rouse you, but the stillness persisted. I wouldn't—couldn't—let this slide. Your health was non-negotiable. We had to know.

We slammed the car door and roared away, the engine's thunder matching the wild pounding in my chest. I hit the radio—WGTS—and for a heartbeat, I desperately waited for "I Believe"[8] to soothe me. Instead, the opening chords of Phil Wickham's "The King Is in the Room"[9] burst through the speakers: "Lift your hands in the Savior's name, there's victory in the air . . ." In that moment, it felt less like music and more like a direct whisper from heaven: *Fear not, the King is with you here.* Yet as we merged onto the freeway, that reassurance battled a hurricane in my mind—every lyric drowned by the ferocity of my fear. The miles stretched into a barren expanse of dread, each second a frantic prayer that God's presence, proclaimed through those words, would hold us together through the darkest drive of our lives.

I reached for Mom's hand, needing her warmth, her reassurance. But her skin was hot, clammy, slick with sweat. I had to pull back, the contact too raw, too real. I glanced at her—her face pale, a single tear rolling down her left cheek, carving a path through her fear. "My God," I prayed, my voice a desperate whisper, "please keep your hands on this child. Bless her, hold her, put your Holy Spirit in her heart." The silence between us was a chasm, filled only with the weight of what might be.

By the time we reached the hospital, my foot was heavy on the gas, each second an eternity. I swerved toward the emergency room door, but Mom's voice cut through the haze. "No," she said, her tone firm yet fragile. "I want to walk in with you."

We parked at the end of the lot in that same awkward create-your-own-spot we'd used before—fate, or perhaps habit, guiding us to the exact same place. I helped Mom out, her steps hesitant but resolute, and together we walked through the emergency room doors. A greeter handed us green labor and delivery stickers, their brightness a stark

---

8   Ibid.
9   Phil Wickham, "The King Is in the Room," written by Phil Wickham, Bethel Music Publishing / Fair Trade Music Publishing, 2009, track 8 on *Heaven & Earth, INO Records, 2009, MP3 audio.*

contrast to the dread in our hearts. We followed the signs, weaving through the building, past familiar faces from past visits—nurses who offered weak smiles and small jokes, trying to lighten the mood, though we both knew the gravity of what we faced.

The elevators carried us to the third floor, where two warm receptionists awaited. Capital Women's Care had called ahead, and the paperwork was nearly ready. As Mom fumbled for her driver's license and insurance, I scribbled my signature on the forms, my hand shaking, each stroke a battle against panic. A triage nurse appeared, ushering Mom away with a promise that I could follow once finished. The separation was torture. *What was happening back there? Was Mom okay? Were you okay?*

The receptionist tried small talk, but I was all business, my mind racing through every nightmare scenario. Finally, I finished and hurried through the hospital maze to Triage Room #8. The sound of the fetal monitor greeted me—its empty, searching tone as the nurse maneuvered it over Mom's belly. "Sash?" I called, hesitant to intrude on the wrong curtain, my voice trembling.

"In here. Follow our voice," the nurse replied. I poked my head in, my heart in my throat.

"Any luck?" I asked, my words barely audible.

"Not yet," she said, her focus intense. My stomach dropped, a cold sweat breaking out across my forehead. Mom's eyes, wide with worry, met mine. She whispered your last known position from the sonogram, guiding the nurse. After a tense, eternal moment of adjustment—there it was. The galloping rhythm of your heart, strong and clear at 172 beats per minute. Relief crashed over us like a tidal wave, Mom's hand squeezing mine as tears spilled from her eyes. For the first time in hours, we breathed.

After ten minutes, your heart rate dipped to 135, then spiked back to 170—a reassuring dance the nurse explained was perfectly normal, a testament to your strength and resilience. "Come on, kid," I murmured, a shaky laugh escaping me. The nurse smiled, detailing your limits, what to watch for, and how healthy you were. But the fear lingered, a shadow we couldn't shake.

The doctor ordered a full physiological exam, so we waited another hour for a sonographer. The nurse wheeled Mom down the corridor in what she jokingly called limousine service, teasing me for my slow pace.

"Conserving energy in case a baby's born," I muttered, but the humor was thin, my arms crossed tightly against the panic still clawing at my chest.

The ultrasound was uneventful—no red flags, no trouble. Another half-hour wait in Triage #8 stretched our nerves thin, but the final doctor's assessment was a balm: All normal, all good. By 5 p.m., we were discharged, the weight of the day pressing down on us. We'd missed Dave's physical therapy, but our neighbor Marcy stepped in, taking him to her place, feeding him dinner, and treating him to ice cream at Jimmy Cone. The kindness of friends shone like a beacon in the darkness.

At home, Mom and I microwaved a simple meal—hot pockets and a Jamaican curry patty—our appetite dulled by the emotional toll. When Dave returned, his eyes wide with tales of ice cream, we both knew we needed a sweet escape too. Braving the chilly March night, we headed to Jimmy Cone ourselves. Mom stayed cozy in the car with heated seats while I shivered in line, the cold a small price for the relief of normalcy.

Mom's next checkup on March 19 at Capital Women's Care brought welcome news. The sonogram showed you practice breathing, your organs fully developed—lungs, kidneys, everything. "She's ready," they said. "If she comes now, no NICU." After a week of terror, this was a lifeline, a sign that we were nearing the end of this ordeal.

Just when we thought the tension had eased, I flew to Michigan on Friday, March 21, to position myself to drive Nana W to Maryland the next day. That evening, Nana W and I joined Josh and Sarah at Oak Pointe Church in Novi, Michigan—a sea of youth and energy, faces I'd never seen but felt an instant connection with. The service began with the Apostles' Creed, and as I recited the words alongside 400 others, my heart sang Phil Wickham's "I Believe":[10]

> *"I believe in God, the Father almighty,*
> *creator of heaven and earth.*
> *I believe in Jesus Christ, his only Son, our Lord,*
> *who was conceived by the Holy Spirit*
> *and born of the virgin Mary..."*

The creed merged with the lyrics in my soul: "I believe there is one salvation... I believe in the name of Jesus Christ... I believe in the crucifixion... I believe in the resurrection... I believe in the hope of heaven..."[11] As the band struck the opening chords of the very song, tears welled in my eyes. In that moment, miles from home, away from my pregnant wife, I felt God's presence, a whisper that I was exactly where I needed to be—and so were you. The song, our battle rhythm through this pregnancy, followed us like a promise.

Through every hardship, medical scares, family quarrels—my faith remains unshaken. I marvel at Mom's strength, her grace in the face of fear. As the sermon ended, I knew one truth: I believe. In God's grace, in His plan for you, in the love that has carried us through every dark hallway and every whispered prayer.

In the days leading to your scheduled c-section, we scurried around, double-checking hospital bags, reorganizing the pantry, ensuring the car seat was secure. Each task was a prayer, each moment borrowed time. Friends from church dropped off meals, and even Colton and Dave tidied their rooms, their excitement intense.

---

10 Phil Wickham, "Battle Belongs."
11 Ibid.

Soon, my love, we will meet. Every tear, every prayer, every breath has been for you.

—Dad

CHAPTER THIRTY-SEVEN

THE DAWN OF YOUR ARRIVAL

March 29, 2025

Eliana,

As the soft glow of dawn gently washed over our bedroom on that early Saturday morning at the beginning of week thirty-eight, I opened my eyes to see the most beautiful woman I've ever laid eyes upon—your mom—peacefully sleeping beside me. She had finally found some rest after weeks of discomfort, while you, my little girl, had finished growing and were now patiently waiting, moving slowly into position for your grand entrance. Mom's hips were aching as they began to widen, making room for you to descend deeper into her abdomen.

In that tranquil moment, I watched her gentle breathing, marveling at how each day of this journey transformed both of us—her body adapting to cradle you, my heart learning a deeper kind of love. Everything felt poised on the edge of a miracle.

My nerves were heightened because I was still on a reserve schedule for March. This meant that at any moment, United could call and send me away on a trip. The idea of missing your birth was unthinkable, yet the threat hung over us. Friday evening was filled with anxiety as several potential assignments loomed, but we dodged them, allowing a brief sigh of relief. However, as Mom and I checked the Bump app

Saturday morning, my phone rang and my heart skipped several beats. The look of panic that flashed across Mom's face mirrored my own as I declined the call from Crew Scheduling, hoping desperately they would move on.

But they called again. Then again. I finally answered the third call, trying to keep my voice steady as Erin, the crew scheduler, asked how soon I could arrive at the airport. Sticking firmly to our union contract, I requested my full two-and-a-half-hour call-out. Despite Erin offering extra pay, I declined to shorten the notice. After a tense pause, she informed me they would delay the flight to accommodate me. I watched Mom's radiant smile fade, replaced by a saddened acceptance as reality set in—I would be gone, possibly missing your birth. My stomach twisted with guilt and worry, yet I reassured her that no matter what, the moment labor started, she could call the flight operations duty manager, and United Airlines would move mountains to bring me home.

Even as my phone buzzed with scheduling details, my mind was with you—picturing Mom unexpectedly going into labor while I was hundreds of miles away. I silently prayed, *God, please hold off. Keep them both safe until I can return.*

Thankfully, the assignment was short: one flight to Cancun, a twenty-four-hour layover, and a return flight to Chicago, then home. Still, being out of the country at such a critical time weighed heavily on my mind. Every hour away felt like days. I checked in with Mom constantly, each conversation filled with reassurances and silent prayers.

On Monday, as I prepared to return home, Mom received a call from the anesthesiologist at Shady Grove Hospital. They explained the details of her spinal procedure for the C-section, cautioning her about potential nausea, shaking, chest pressure, and breathlessness—all normal, but still daunting. The nurse mentioned they had medication and ice ready in case her tachycardia flared up during surgery. That call made the reality of your imminent arrival vividly clear.

Monday afternoon, anxiety returned as our flight from Cancun was routed around a storm over the Gulf of America, pushing our arrival into Chicago to seventeen minutes late. Every minute counted, as I had exactly an hour and thirty-one minutes to clear Customs, switch terminals, re-clear security, and board my connecting flight home. Yet, amid the stress, Philippians 4:6-7 echoed reassuringly in my mind: *"Don't worry about anything; instead, pray about everything. Tell God what you need and thank him for all he has done. Then you will experience God's peace, which exceeds anything we can understand. His peace will guard your hearts and minds as you live in Christ Jesus."*[12] With a deep breath, I surrendered my worries to God. Miraculously, I cleared Customs quickly, caught the train, and reached my gate with plenty of time. As I boarded, I texted Mom, "It's okay to have the baby now, I'll be home in an hour." Her laughter filled my heart, and we both exhaled deeply, knowing that I'd be there for your arrival.

I couldn't help smiling at the way God orchestrates details. Even storms seemed to step aside just enough to make sure I'd be beside you and Mom when it mattered most.

Your final weeks were undoubtedly the hardest for Mom. Though filled with joy, her every step revealed exhaustion. From 10 p.m. to 4 a.m. every night, you danced tirelessly in her belly, ensuring sleep was a luxury she rarely experienced. She spent restless nights shifting to her left side to ease discomfort and breathe easier, her body tirelessly working for your arrival.

As week thirty-eight closed, we attended Mom's final OB appointment. The ultrasound was quick and routine. Dr. Spector, known for her cheerful banter in the operating room, reassured Mom, easing some anxieties about the surgery. Driving home, we reminisced about the last eleven months—from fertility shots and nervous anticipation to the miraculous embryo transfer. Upon arriving home, the hospital called, meticulously outlining procedures for your birth day. Mom humorously asked when she could finally eat a ham sandwich again,

---
12 Philippians 4:6-7 New Living Translation (NLT).

eager to end her eleven-month deli-meat prohibition. That night, after settling into our Netflix show, I drifted off quickly, oblivious to Mom quietly battling contractions and soothing herself with a late-night bath. When she casually mentioned it the next morning, my heart raced at the thought you might arrive earlier than planned, tears of excitement threatening to spill as I dropped Colton off at school.

It struck me how every detail—down to the types of foods she missed—was a reminder of the sacrifices she made for your sake. Each time she sighed about wanting that ham sandwich, I sensed the warmth of her love for you shining through.

The weekend preceding your birth was filled with preparations. Nana W was already with us, offering comfort and support. Mom spent Saturday finalizing every detail, and I took Colton for a haircut while Nana W prepared a wonderful dinner. On Sunday morning, Nana W, Colton, and I visited the breathtaking cherry blossoms in DC, capturing serene beauty before our world changed forever. Meanwhile, Mom indulged in self-care, echoing the day our IVF journey began: a manicure, pedicure, fresh haircut, and new hair color, ensuring she looked her absolute best for the arrival of her little princess.

As your final week—week thirty-nine—arrived, you were considered full term. According to the Bump, you were roughly nineteen to twenty-one inches long and about seven to eight pounds. Your brain and lungs were fully mature, and you were ready for the world. Mom's body prepared intensely, her hips expanding, and her discomfort intensifying, each movement a reminder of your nearing birth.

The Calm Before the Storm

March 30, 2025

Sunday night, as the final preparations wrapped up, the hospital's instructions echoed in our minds: labs at 10 a.m., arrive at Labor and Delivery by 10:30. Mom joked about how she couldn't wait for a ham sandwich—anything to replace the hospital's endless lime Jell-o. As we settled into bed one final time as a family of four, our hearts overflowed with anticipation. The house was still and hushed, as if holding its breath for morning to come. Suitcases were lined up by the door, and the car was already packed with everything we needed for the hospital.

All that remained was to get through these last few hours of darkness before we finally met you, our precious daughter. In the soft glow of our bedroom lamp, I could see both stress and relief mingling in your mom's eyes. The end was near—just one more night until the day that would change our lives forever. My heart ached with anticipation as I made my way to the bed, quietly praying for courage.

Mom gave me a small, tired smile—both of us fully aware that whatever worries, aches, or fears lingered, we were about to step into the moment we'd been waiting for. It felt like standing on holy ground, each second sacred and charged with the promise of meeting you.

Sitting down next to your mom, I felt a rush of emotion. I had wanted to share prayer with her for so long, but something inside me hesitated. My faith in God always felt so personal—like a sacred bond I wasn't sure how to let another person into. I feared it might somehow weaken my connection with Him. Silly, perhaps, but very real to me at the time. Yet the closer we got to your birth, the stronger my desire grew to weave God directly into our marriage, not just our individual lives. In the weeks leading up to that night, I prayed often for the courage to open my spiritual life to your mom. One evening, while on the road, I was lying in bed and scrolling through Facebook when I stumbled upon a string of Christian videos—messages that felt heaven-sent. Among them was a short sermon by a young pastor that spoke so deeply to my heart, I immediately recognized it as God's answer to my prayers.

According to data often attributed to the National Association of Marriage Enhancement and cited in various Christian marriage resources, couples who pray together regularly are significantly less likely to divorce. While exact figures vary, the message is clear: Shared spiritual practice builds unity. Ecclesiastes 4: 9–12 reminds us that "a cord of three strands is not easily broken"—a beautiful picture of God's presence strengthening the bond between husband and wife.

Three Chords: God as the Unbreakable Strand

He led me to Ecclesiastes 4:9–12, which says:

> *"Two people are better off than one, for they can help each other succeed. If one person falls, the other can reach out and help. But someone who falls alone is in real trouble. Likewise, two people lying close together can keep each other warm. But how can one be warm alone? A person standing alone can be attacked and defeated, but two can stand back-to-back and conquer. Three are even better, for a triple-braided cord is not easily broken."*[13]

To illustrate this, imagine braiding hair—an image that immediately brought clarity to my heart:

1. **Two Strands Alone**
   When you take two sections of hair and twist them together, they might hold briefly, but as soon as there's wind or movement, they begin to unravel. In marriage, disagreements, unexpected heartbreaks, and life's relentless pressures tug at those two strands. With enough strain, they loosen, and then unravel completely.

2. **Adding the Third Strand**
   Now picture introducing a third section of hair—a strong, consistent thread woven from the scalp to the tips. Suddenly, the braid stays tight and holds firm regardless of how much you move or how hard the wind blows. Nothing can easily pry it apart because all three strands support each other.

---

[13] Ecclesiastes 4:9–12, New Living Translation (NLT).

3. **God as Our Third Cord**
   In marriage, God is that unbreakable third strand. When we invite Him to be an active, guiding presence—not just in each of our individual lives but in our shared life—He strengthens our bond against every trial. This doesn't guarantee an effortless journey, but it does promise a supernatural resilience rooted in grace, love, and faithfulness.

4. **A Marriage Without the Third Strand**
   If a couple keeps God at a distance—both individually knowing Him, but never actively praying together—it's as though two strands of hair lie beside a spool of thread without ever being woven together. The strands remain separate, susceptible to snapping or fraying under pressure.

5. **Weaving God Into Our Lives**
   True strength emerges when we interlace God into the very fabric of our relationship—through prayer, unity, and intentional surrender. Just as a tightly woven braid remains intact from top to bottom, so does a marriage fortified by God endure from one stage of life to the next.

This sermon made me realize I didn't need to protect my personal faith from your mom; I needed to share it with her. God belonged not just in our individual hearts but also at the core of our relationship.

The First Prayer Together

So, that Sunday night, as the house settled and the final countdown to your birth began, I looked at your mom, my heart thudding in my chest, and gently asked, "Can we pray together?"

Her eyes lit up with a smile that banished every lingering hesitation I had. We settled on the edge of the bed, knee to knee, our fingers intertwined. Bowing our heads until our cheeks nearly touched, I spoke:

"Heavenly Father,

Thank You for the precious gift of Eliana and for guiding us through this incredible journey. Tonight, I lift up Sasha to You—cover her in peace, strength, and protection as she prepares to bring our daughter into the world.

Surround the medical team with wisdom and steady hands. Let this cesarean birth be safe, smooth, and full of Your presence.

Lord, I also pray for Eliana—our miracle, our answered prayer. Watch over her as she takes her first breath. Guard her health, her heart, and her future. May she grow in strength, wisdom, and grace, walking boldly in Your purpose for her life.

Let her life be filled with joy, love, and divine protection all her days."

In that moment, I felt a burden lift; an indescribable peace and joy filled the room. Tears shimmered in your mom's eyes as she thanked me for the prayer, and I realized that sharing faith with my wife didn't weaken my relationship with God; it made it stronger.

I promised your mom that night we would continue to pray together, to keep God woven into our marriage as our third, unbreakable cord. The peace in our room was almost tangible—an undeniable presence of the Holy Spirit moving between us. We switched off the lamp, hearts brimming with a new kind of closeness.

Tomorrow, we'd walk into the hospital hand in hand, ready to meet you—our shining miracle. We would do it as a team of three strands, interlaced by faith, hope, and the everlasting love of our Father in Heaven. And that's how our final evening before your birth came to a close: Not with fear or worry but in the warmth of prayer and the promise that our marriage—like a well-braided cord—would hold strong against any storm.

I breathed one last prayer that night, whispering thanks for everything—every tear, every shot, every hospital run—knowing we were mere hours away from meeting the little girl we had believed in for so long.

Tomorrow, March 31, 2025, you will grace this world, Eliana José María. Your arrival marks the culmination of prayers, struggles, and immense faith. Your name carries the legacy of those we've loved and lost, and your presence will fill our lives with unimaginable joy. Tonight, as the house settles into peaceful anticipation, we rest in the knowledge that tomorrow, our greatest miracle arrives.

We love you endlessly, my sweet girl. We will meet you tomorrow.

With all our hearts,

Dad

CHAPTER THIRTY EIGHT

"GOD HAS ANSWERED — I BELIEVE"

March 31, 2025 began with the first gentle glow of sunrise at 7:45 a.m., a soft warmth spilling through our bedroom window that felt like a whisper of destiny. Your mother—my rock throughout this entire journey—slept beside me, her face calm, unaware of just how profoundly our lives would change today. My heart pounded with anticipation, love, and a touch of fear. We had prayed for this moment, dreamed of it through every hurdle, and now it was here: The day we would finally meet you, our precious Eliana.

Something in the morning light felt almost sacred, as if time itself were pausing to witness this new chapter unfolding.

At 9:17 a.m., we were standing at the threshold of our home, ready to leave for the hospital. In that moment, time felt slower, as if lingering to let us say goodbye to our familiar world. Your brothers, Colton and Dave, gave us clumsy hugs and kisses, their eyes glittering with an unspoken blend of curiosity and concern. Both of your Nanas circled us like guardian angels, making sure we had every last detail covered—extra blankets, phone chargers, the camera, the car seat.

Just outside the mudroom, on the way to the car, I paused on the sidewalk, struck by a sudden rush of emotion. *This is it,* I thought.

The last time we'll leave this house as a family of four. Tears stung at my eyes. Your mom, sensing my hesitation, turned back with that gentle smile I've loved for years. She wrapped me in a comforting hug and asked, "Everything okay?" In her embrace, the swirl of emotions—excitement, fear, bittersweet anticipation—seemed to calm. Together, we took a deep breath and settled into the car, the clock reading 9:20.

I cautiously backed out of the driveway at 9:20 a.m., fully aware this was our final drive to the hospital before meeting you. My heart fluttered with a mix of excitement and nerves as I flipped through the radio stations, hoping to hear the familiar opening notes of "I Believe." Our neighborhood, usually humming with its own rhythm, felt eerily still—almost as if everything beyond our car had paused out of reverence for the moment.

I couldn't help but recall every hospital visit, every prayer, every injection that had led us here. With each mile we drove, a piece of our past unspooled behind us, clearing the way for your arrival.

Your mom and I exchanged glances every few seconds, neither of us quite trusting our voices not to crack under the weight of this day. She stroked her belly absently, and I noticed how she winced if you made an especially big kick. Her face was a combination of excitement and serene resolve—her countdown had ended, and this was it.

I continued to distract myself by turning on the radio, cycling through three Christian stations and silently praying our anthem, "I Believe," would somehow cut through the noise. The crackle of commercials and sermon snippets only stoked my nerves further. I realized I was gripping the steering wheel so tightly that my knuckles had turned white.

At one point, I glanced at the dashboard clock—9:35 a.m.—and caught your mother's gaze. We both laughed, a quiet, breathy sound. It felt surreal to think that in less than an hour, we'd be at the hospital, well on our way to meeting you. Yet, the laughter was tinged with nerves. The labor of an entire pregnancy—physically, emotionally, spiritually—was about to culminate.

Moments later, lost in thought, I noticed I exited the freeway 1 exit too soon. Startled, I let out a quick expletive, and your mother chuckled. "It's okay," she said, her voice brimming with encouragement. "Just get back on right here." I took the next exit, looping back around to correct my course, feeling a mixture of embarrassment and relief. It struck me that, in a few hours, none of these little slip-ups would matter at all.

Finally, I surrendered to technology. While stopped at a red light, I pulled out my phone and tapped on Apple Music, selecting our cherished track. Phil Wickham's "I Believe" poured through the speakers, and instantly, I could feel the tension in my shoulders ease. I caught your mother smiling—a real, full smile this time—as she pressed her hand to her stomach. Right then, as though you recognized your own theme song, you began to kick with renewed vigor. "Feel that?" your mom whispered, eyes shining. I placed a hand over hers, my heart pounding at the flurry of movement inside.

The highway ahead unfurled in a short, one-mile stretch, and the sun broke through scattered clouds, throwing patches of light across the asphalt. With "I Believe" echoing in the car, I felt a sudden surge of confidence. God had carried us through so many storms—why would He fail us now? The final chorus soared just as we pulled into Shady Grove Hospital at 9:55 a.m., a wave of calm settling over us that felt almost supernatural.

We found a spot close to the entrance and let the engine idle for a moment, allowing the last notes of the song to fade into a gentle hush. Your mother reached for my hand across the console, her eyes reflecting both anticipation and serenity. Neither of us needed words. The drive—its nerves, its stumbles—mirrored our entire journey: moments of fear and confusion, ultimately guided back on course by faith and love.

At exactly 10:00 a.m., we stepped out of the car. The hush of that moment seemed to echo our reverence for the day's significance.

With one final, mutual nod of resolve, we walked through the sliding doors of Shady Grove Hospital, crossing into the threshold of your long-awaited arrival.

Your mom and I walked into Shady Grove, arms linked and hearts pounding with anticipation. Hospital workers along the corridor offered cheerful greetings and well wishes—congratulating your mom as we headed toward Labor and Delivery. She practically glowed with happiness; I could see it in every step she took, Eliana. At the registration desk, the clerk smiled at my stack of pre-filled forms and joked about our meticulous preparation. We laughed, relief settling over us; everything felt so wonderfully right—we were finally ready.

We didn't wait long—only about ten minutes—before a nurse guided us through a maze of hallways to Room 23. In that small, bright space, our journey to meet you ramped up. First came the IV, though the nurse had trouble finding a good vein. Your mother gripped my hand like a lifeline; the pain etched across her face made me wish I could bear it for her. After the nurse switched to her other hand, the IV finally found its mark, and we breathed a collective sigh of relief. One more step complete, one inch closer to holding you in our arms.

By 11:45, the anesthesiologist arrived, calmly explaining how everything would work to keep your mother comfortable for the surgery. Moments later, Dr. Spector entered to review the risks of a cesarean, including the word "death." My stomach clenched; despite our faith, that single word cut through my composure. One tear escaped, and I quickly wiped it away. Your mom, steady as a rock, turned her gaze on me: "It's going to be okay," she whispered, "Papito will be with me." Still, I knew she was just as frightened beneath that calm exterior. Before the team left, she recorded a short video message for you—a tender, final snapshot of her love during the last moments you spent together, connected.

I felt that familiar mixture of awe and vulnerability wash over me—how close we were to our dream, yet also how precarious life can feel in the final hours before birth.

Shortly after 12:35, a group of nurses arrived to escort your mother to the operating room. I leaned over, pressed a gentle kiss on her forehead, and whispered one more "I love you" before they guided me to the post-op holding area. There, I slipped into a white medical suit, foot covers, and a hairnet. Suddenly alone, I felt every swirl of emotion crash over me—excitement to meet you, dread of the unknown, unshakable faith that God would protect us. In an attempt to calm my racing heart, I played our song, "I Believe,"[14] letting it fill my headphones while I wrote down every frantic thought, every desperate prayer for your safe arrival.

Time dragged on. Finally, at 12:57, a nurse reappeared, beckoning me with a smile. "Dad, it's time," she said. My chest tightened as I texted your brother Colton, your Nana W, and your Papa:

> *"Here we go 😬 . Sasha is all prepped, numb, and in the OR. I'm walking back now. Pray for Sasha. I'm scared for her."*

The operating room was bright, sterile, and humming with the soft mechanical whirs of medical equipment. Your mother lay on the table, appearing far braver than I knew she felt inside. I took a seat beside her, held her hand, and whispered, "Papito is right here, holding your hand." We prayed under our breath, finding small moments of humor to chase away the tension. I could hear the doctors conversing, instruments clinking as they worked. From my vantage point, I caught glimpses of the operation in the reflection of a cabinet door—a surreal image, like watching a scene from someone else's life unfold.

Then came a sudden gush of fluid and the sight of deep red. I asked, half in awe, "Did her water just break?" A nurse nodded. My heart hammered, realizing we were seconds away from the climax of months—years—of longing and faith. Sure enough, within moments, the air erupted with the purest, most triumphant sound: Your first cry. It was a clarion call of life. Tears sprang to my eyes as the doctors lowered a small window in the drape so your mom could see you.

---

14 Phil Wickham, *"I Believe."*

"Time of birth, 1:07," someone announced, though the words barely registered over my pounding heartbeat.

I had my phone ready, capturing those first precious moments as they laid you against your mother's chest. You seemed to nestle into her immediately, your cries subsiding just enough for you two to share your first "hello." The doctors invited me over to see you more closely; I glanced at your mom for permission, and she gave an eager nod. My heart felt like it was on fire as I crossed the room.

They set you on a tiny scale, zeroing it out. "Seven pounds, seven ounces," a nurse declared. 1:07 p.m., I mentally repeated. 7-7-1:07—a pattern that felt almost too perfect, like God's personal signature on your birth. A wave of disappointment struck me briefly when I realized your umbilical cord was already cut—I'd missed that ritual with your brother, too—but the second I laid eyes on you, all sadness vanished. You were just so perfect. The nurse handed you to me, and I bent to kiss your forehead, my voice cracking, "Hi, princess." In that instant, my entire being overflowed with a love I cannot begin to put into words.

Cradling you securely, I walked back to your mother's side. She was still being stitched up, but her tears of joy outshone every worry. "Thank you, Papito," she whispered, the two of us in silent awe of you. I offered a prayer of gratitude and protection, asking God to watch over you both. It was one of the holiest moments of my life.

Once the surgery wrapped up, the nurses transferred your mother and you to the post anesthesia care unit (PACU). I followed closely, never letting you out of my sight. Over the next two hours, they monitored your mother's vitals post-surgery and checked you over—administering your first shots, applying antibiotic ointment to protect your eyes. Each moment felt dreamlike, as I tried to split my attention between your mother's well-being and the mesmerizing wonder of you. Eventually, about three hours after your birth, we were settled into the Mother–Baby wing, where we could finally exhale and share our first quiet moments together as a family.

Those next few days blurred into a tapestry of late-night feedings, gentle lullabies, and hushed conversations between your mother and me. You took to breastfeeding almost effortlessly, bringing immense relief after all the stories we'd heard of newborn struggles. On April 3, 2025, at 3:25 p.m., we carried you out of the hospital and brought you home—a place already brimming with love and eager arms ready to hold you.

Eliana, our road to you was long and steep, fraught with countless prayers, tears, and doubts. But always, at every twist and turn, God gave us the strength to press on, reminding us to trust in His plan. And so, with the faith that carried us through many storms, we declare:

> "I believe there is one salvation
> One doorway that leads to life
> One redemption, one confession
> I believe in the name of Jesus Christ."[15]

Your story, Eliana, isn't just ours to cherish; it's a beacon of hope for anyone walking the uncertain path of fertility. You are living proof that God's grace can outshine every setback and calm every storm. From our very first prayer to this triumphant moment, He guided us steadily, reminding us at every turn that you were worth every trial we endured. May your life continue to mirror that unshakeable faith, and may you always know you were cherished beyond measure from the moment your existence was only a dream. Welcome to the world, sweet girl—you are, and always will be, our beautiful testament to the power of hope and the promise of God's unfailing love.

God has answered. I Believe.

---

15   Ibid

OUR BLENDED FAMILY TREE

Papa Wheeler
Papa

Nana Wheeler
Nana W

Jose Maria
Papito

Nana Mihalikova
Nana M

Aunt Nicki

Jeffrey
Dad

Aunt Jenni

Sasha
Mom

Colton
CJ

Warren
Ren/Dave

Eliana
Jose Maria

www.ingramcontent.com/pod-product-compliance
Lightning Source LLC
LaVergne TN
LVHW061046070526
838201LV00074B/5199